The New York Historical Society

1804-1904

BY

ROBERT HENDRE KELBY

LIBRARIAN OF THE SOCIETY

NEW YORK

PUBLISHED FOR THE SOCIETY

MDCCCCV

INTRODUCTION

The studies for this brief history were prepared for a paper read by Mr. Kelby on November 1, 1904, as a retrospect of the century which had elapsed since the foundation of the Society. The present volume includes the chief points of the "Retrospect," and an appendix gives a list of the publications of the Society and other details of interest in its history.

Daniel Parish, Jr.,
Frederic Wendell Jackson,
Robert H. Kelby,
Committee on Publications.

CONTENTS

ILLUSTRATIONS

Minutes
of the
New York Historical Society.

New York, Novr 20th 1804

The following Persons viz. Egbert Benson, DeWitt Clinton, Revd William Linn, Revd Samuel Miller, Revd John N. Abeel, Revd John M. Mason, [illegible], Doctor David Hosack, Anthony Bleecker, Samuel Bayard, Peter Stuyvesant and John Pintard, being assembled in the Picture Room of the City Hall of the City of New York, agreed to form themselves into a Society the principal designs of which should be to collect and preserve whatever may relate to the natural, civil or ecclesiastical History of the United States in general and of this State in particular and appointed Mr. Benson, Doctor Miller and Mr. Pintard a Committee to prepare and report a draft of a Constitution.

The Meeting then adjourned until Monday evening the 10th of December next.

FOUNDERS OF THE SOCIETY

THE NEW YORK HISTORICAL SOCIETY

1804–1904

THE plan for the organization of this institution originated with John Pintard, through whose exertions several meetings for the purpose were held in a room of the City Hall, Wall Street, in 1804. After canvassing the matter for some time, the persons who had been invited to take part in the preliminary arrangements appointed a committee to draft a constitution, under which an organization finally took place.

The minutes of the Society contain the following record of the first meeting:

"NEW YORK, November 20, 1804.

The following persons, vizt.—Egbert Benson, DeWitt Clinton, Rev. William Linn, Rev. Samuel Miller, Rev. John N. Abeel, Rev. John M. Mason, Doctor David Hosack, Anthony Bleecker, Samuel Bayard, Peter G. Stuyvesant, and John Pintard, being assembled in the Picture Room of the City Hall of the City of New York, agreed to form themselves into a Society, the principal design of which should be to collect and preserve whatever may relate to the natural, civil or ecclesiastical History of the United States in general, and of this State in particular, and appointed Mr. Benson, Doctor Miller, and Mr. Pintard a committee to prepare and report a draft of a Constitution."

The meeting then adjourned until Monday evening, December 10th, following.

At this meeting the following gentlemen were present:

EGBERT BENSON, *Chairman.*

De Witt Clinton,	Rev. John C. Kunze,
Rev. John M. Mason,	Rev. Samuel Miller,
Rev. John Bowden,	Dr. Peter Wilson,
Rev. Wiliam Harris,	Peter G. Stuyvesant,
Dr. John Kemp,	John Murray, Jr.,
Daniel D. Tompkins,	Rev. John H. Hobart,
Rufus King,	Dr. David Hosack,
Rev. John N. Abeel,	Dr. Archibald Bruce,

John Pintard.

A constitution was adopted, and the institution was named "The New York Historical Society."

The first regular meeting after the adoption of the constitution was held January 14, 1805, at which time the Society was organized by the election of the following

OFFICERS:

EGBERT BENSON, *President.*

RT. REV. BENJAMIN MOORE, D.D.,
First Vice-President.

BROCKHOLST LIVINGSTON,
Second Vice-President.

REV. SAMUEL MILLER, D.D.,
Corresponding Secretary.

JOHN PINTARD, *Recording Secretary.*

CHARLES WILKES, *Treasurer.*

JOHN FORBES, *Librarian.*

STANDING COMMITTEE

WILLIAM JOHNSON, DANIEL D. TOMPKINS,
DR. SAML. L. MITCHILL, JOHN MCKESSON,
DR. DAVID HOSACK, ANTHONY BLEECKER,
REV. JOHN M. MASON, D.D.

A Seal was adopted, and later a Vignette for Diploma, by Durand, showing the arrival of Henry Hudson, 1609.

The following short sketch of the lives of the eleven gentlemen who first met on Tuesday, November 20, 1804, may prove interesting:

EGBERT BENSON, first president of the Society was born in this city, June 21, 1746, and died in Jamaica, L. I., August 24, 1833. He was the first

Attorney General of the State, 1777-89, a member of the Continental Congress, 1784-88, and was returned to the First and to the Second Congress. He was Judge of the Supreme Court of New York, 1794-1802, and member of Congress again, 1813-15. He delivered before the Society, December 31, 1816, a memoir on Dutch names of places. Judge Benson served as president until 1815, when he declined a reëlection.

De Witt Clinton, vice-president, 1810-16; president of the Society, 1817-19, was born near Little Britain, N. Y., March 2, 1769; died at Albany, February 11, 1828; was graduated from Columbia College, 1786; private secretary to his uncle, Gov. George Clinton, 1790-95; member of Assembly, 1797, and of the State Senate, 1798-1802 and 1806-11; United States Senator, 1802-03; Mayor of this city, 1803-07, 1809-10, and 1811—15, and by his wise and efficient administration contributed much to the prosperity of the city; one of the founders of this Society and the Academy of Fine Arts; first president of the Literary and Philosophical Society; Lieutenant-Governor of this State, 1811-13, and Governor of the State, 1817-22 and 1824-27; initiated the construction of the Erie Canal, 1815; Canal Commissioner, 1816, 1823-24. The opening of the Erie Canal was celebrated with a great demonstration in October, 1825, Gov. Clinton was conveyed in a barge on a triumphal progress from Lake Erie to this city, and on November 4th following proceeded down the bay to the ocean, when Clinton with great solemnity poured from an elegant keg adorned with many devices and inscriptions, and gilded hoops, the waters of Lake Erie into the Atlantic Ocean. The keg, preserved as a precious memento of the interesting ceremony, is in the possession of this Society. Clinton delivered the anniversary discourse before the Society in 1811, which was published.

Rev. William Linn, D.D., was born in Shippensburg, Pa., February 27, 1752; son of William and Susanna (Trimble) Linn, and grandson of William Linn, who with his son William came from the north of Ireland in 1732, and settled in the township of Lurgan, Cumberland County, Pa. William 3d was graduated at the College of New Jersey, 1772; studied theology with the Rev. Dr. Robert Cooper, and was chaplain of the Fifth and Sixth Battalions, Continental army. He was pastor of the Presbyterian church, Big Spring (Newville), Pa., 1777-84; at Elizabethtown, N. J., 1784-85; of the Collegiate Dutch Reformed church, New York city, 1787-1805; president *pro tempore* of Rutgers College, 1791-94, and trustee 1787-1808; regent of the University of the State of New York, 1787-1808; chaplain of the House of Representatives, First Congress, 1789-91, and was elected president of Union College, Schenectady, N. Y., in 1804, but not inaugurated. He received the degree of D.D. from the College of New Jersey in 1789. He was married first to Rebecca, daughter of the Rev.

John Blair, vice-president of the College of New Jersey; secondly to Mrs. Catherine Moore, widow of Dr. Moore, of New York city; and thirdly to Helen Hanson. He is the author of "Sermons" (1791), "Signs of the Times" (1794), "Funeral Eulogy on Washington" (1800), and "Sermon on the Death of Alexander Hamilton" (1804). He died in Albany, N, Y., January 8, 1808.

Rev. Samuel Miller, D.D., corresponding secretary of the Society, 1805-13, was born near Dover, Del., October 31, 1769; son of the Rev. John and Margaret (Millington) Miller; grandson of Allumby and Elizabeth (Harris) Millington, of Talbot County, Md., and of John Miller, a Scotchman, who immigrated to Boston, Mass., in 1719, where he married Margaret Bass, of Braintree. Samuel received his preparatory education under his father; entered the senior class of the University of Pennsylvania, and was graduated there with first honors, 1789. He was licensed to preach by the Presbytery of Lewes, Del., October 13, 1791, shortly after his father's death, and completed his theological studies under the Rev. Charles Nisbet in 1792. He preached in several churches in Delaware; was a colleague to the Rev. Dr. Rodgers and the Rev. Dr. McKnight in the "Brick" and "Wall Street" church, known then as the First Church, New York city, 1793-1809, and sole pastor of the Wall Street church, 1809-13. He was married October 24, 1801, to Sarah, daughter of the Hon. Jonathan Dickinson and Margaret (Spencer) Sergeant, of Philadelphia, Pa. He was moderator of the General Assembly of the Presbyterian Church in 1806; a founder and director of Princeton Theological Seminary, 1812-13, and Professor of Ecclesiastical History and Church Government there 1813-49, and professor emeritus 1849-50. He was commissioned by Governor Tompkins chaplain of the First Regiment of the New York Artillery in April, 1809. He made strong efforts to promote peace between the two factions of the Presbyterian Church. He declined the presidency of the University of North Carolina and of Hamilton College in 1812. He was a trustee of Columbia College, 1806-13, and of the College of New Jersey, 1807-50. He became a member of the American Philosophical Society in 1800; a corresponding member of the Philosophical Society of Manchester, England, 1804; and a corresponding member of the Massachusetts and New Jersey Historical Societies. He received the honorary degree A.M. from Yale and the College of New Jersey in 1792; D.D. from the University of Pennsylvania and Union College in 1804, and from the University of North Carolina in 1811, and LL.D. from Washington College, Maryland, in 1847. He published over forty political and religious pamphlets. He died in Princeton, N. J., January 7, 1850.

REV. JOHN NEILSON ABEEL, D.D., was born in New York city in 1769. His father, James Abeel, was a major in the Revolutionary army, and served through the war as deputy quartermaster-general. The family descended from Christian Janse Abeel, who was born in Amsterdam in 1631, but came to this country and settled in Albany in 1657. Dr. Abeel's mother, from whom he derived his middle name, was the daughter of an Irish gentleman, John Neilson, M.D., who came from Belfast and practised his profession with success in this city. Dr. Abeel early in life was sent to school in Morristown, N. J., where he was fitted for college. He graduated from Princeton in 1787. He studied law in New Brunswick, in the office of the Hon. William Paterson, LL.D., who afterward became one of the Justices of the Supreme Court of the United States. Later he determined to abandon the law and study for the ministry. Accordingly, he entered his name as a student of theology in the Reformed Dutch Church. Soon afterward, however, he was induced to accept an appointment as a tutor in Princeton, and, while thus employed (1791-93), prosecuted his theological studies under the direction of Dr. Witherspoon, the president of the college. His license to preach was granted to him in April, 1793. Shortly after he entered in the service of the Second and Third Presbyterian churches in Philadelphia. He was called to the Collegiate Church at New York in June, 1795, to become one of its ministers. Here he continued to labor during the rest of his life, although he was frequently asked to go elsewhere. He took a lively interest in educational matters, and in 1799 was elected a trustee of Columbia College, and in 1808 a trustee of Queen's College, and once was called to the presidency of Union College. His degree of D.D. was conferred by Harvard College in 1804. Dr. Abeel married January 29, 1794, Mary Stillé, in Philadelphia. She survived her husband a number of years, and died in New York, January 13, 1826, universally esteemed. They had five children, two of whom died in infancy. In 1809 Dr. Abeel's health began to fail, and he died January 19, 1812.

REV. JOHN MITCHELL MASON, D.D., was born in New York city, March 19, 1770; son of the Rev. John and Catherine (Van Wyck) Mason. He was prepared for college under his father; was graduated at Columbia in 1789; was a student in the University of Scotland, 1791-92, and was recalled to the United States by the death of his father in 1792. He was licensed by the Associate Reformed Presbytery of Pennsylvania, October 18, 1792, and installed as pastor of the Cedar Street Church, New York city, as successor to his father, in April, 1793. He was married May 13, 1793, to Ann, daughter of Abraham Lefferts, of New York city. He visited Scotland in 1801, to obtain competent evangelical ministers for duty in the United States, and in September, 1802, proposed a theological seminary, subject to the direction of the Associate Reformed Church, which movement resulted in the Union Theological Seminary. He established the *Christian Magazine* in

January, 1807, and edited it for several years. He resigned his pastorate in 1810, formed a new congregation, and, while a new church was being built, held meetings in the Presbyterian church on Cedar Street. This action resulted in a charge being brought against him at the meeting of the synod in Philadelphia in 1811, but the synod refused to censure him. He was a trustee of Columbia College, 1795-1821, and provost, 1811-16; travelled in France, Italy, and Switzerland, 1816-17, and resigned his pastoral duties in February, 1821, on account of his increasing infirmities. He was president of Dickinson College, Carlisle, Pa., 1821-24, and in 1822 transferred his relations from the Associate Reformed Church to the Presbytery of New York, and returned to New York city in 1824. He received the degree of A.M. from the College of New Jersey in 1794, and that of D.D. from the University of Pennsylvania in 1804. Author of many essays, orations, and sermons. He died in New York city, December 26, 1829.

David Hosack, corresponding secretary, 1814-16; vice-president, 1817-18; president of the Society, 1820-27; was born in New York city, August 31, 1769; son of Alexander and Jane (Arden) Hosack. His father was a native of Moray County, Scotland, who came to America as an artillery officer, serving in the capture of Louisburg in 1758. His maternal grandfather, Francis Arden, was a prominent citizen of New York city. David was a student at Columbia College, 1786-88, and was attacked by the "Doctor's Mob." He graduated at the College of New Jersey, 1789, studied medicine with Drs. Post, Romeyn, Bard, Moore, and Kissam, and received his M.D. degree from the University of Pennsylvania in 1791, and from Edinburgh in 1793. He was married to Catharine Warner, of Princeton, N. J., in 1791. He practised medicine in Alexandria, Va., 1791-92; was a student at Edinburgh and London, 1792-94; and professor of botany, 1795-1811, and of materia medica, 1796-1811, in Columbia College. He was married a second time, December 21, 1797, to Mary, daughter of James and Mary (Darragh) Eddy, of Philadelphia. He attended Alexander Hamilton in his duel with Aaron Burr in 1804. He established in 1822 a hospital, which afterward became Bellevue, and in 1826 joined with Dr. Valentine Mott and Dr. John W. Francis in founding the medical department of Rutgers College, in which he was professor during its existence, 1826-30. He was president of the Horticultural, Literary and Philosophical societies, and originated and in 1801 established the Elgin Botanic Garden, the second in the United States. He was married a third time, shortly before he retired from practice, to Magdalina, widow of Henry A. Coster, a Holland merchant, and spent his summers on his estate at Hyde-Park-on-Hudson, N. Y., where he devoted himself to botanical study. He was expert in the treatment of yellow fever. He received the honorary degree of

LL.D., from the College of New Jersey and from Union College in 1818. He was the author of many medical and scientific works. He died in New York city, December 22, 1835.

ANTHONY BLEECKER, second vice-president of the Society, 1820, was born in New York city in October, 1770; son of Anthony Lispenard Bleecker. His father owned a large estate in New York city. In 1791 he was graduated from Columbia College, and subsequently was admitted to the bar. Preferring literary work to the practice of law, he became well known as a contributor of both prose and verse to current literature. He published the "Narrative of the Brig Commerce," which had a wide circulation. In 1810 he was elected a trustee of the New York Society Library, retaining the office until the year before his death, which occurred March 13, 1827. He was a member of the standing committee of the Society 1805-19 and 1821-27.

SAMUEL BAYARD was born in Philadelphia, Pa., January 11, 1767; the fourth son of John and Margaret (Hodge) Bayard. After his graduation from Princeton College, in 1784, as valedictorian, he studied law and established an excellent practice in his native city. He became interested and prominent in politics, and was made Clerk of the Supreme Court of the United States in 1791. From 1794 to 1798 he represented the United States Government in London, as its agent, to prosecute American claims before the admiralty courts. Upon his return he practised law at New Rochelle, N. Y., receiving the appointment of Presiding Judge of Westchester County. From 1803 to 1806 he resided and practised in New York city. He aided in the organization of the American Bible Society and the New Jersey Bible Society. He removed to Princeton, N. J., in 1806, and was a member of the House of Assembly. He died in Princeton, N. J., May 12, 1840.

PETER GERARD STUYVESANT, great-great-grandson of Governor Petrus Stuyvesant, was born in New York city, 1778; graduated at Columbia College, 1794; studied law and was admitted to the bar. He was elected president of the Society in 1836, and served in that office until 1839. He died at Niagara Falls, N. Y., August 16, 1847. His residence, "Petersfield," was built before the revolution, and was situated on his father's "Bouwerie" farm.

JOHN PINTARD, founder of the Society, was born in New York city, May 18, 1759; son of John and Mary (Cannon) Pintard; grandson of John and Catharine (Carré) Pintard and of John Cannon (father of Le Grand Cannon, of Canada), and great-grandson of Anthony Pintard, a Huguenot, who settled at Shrewsbury in 1786, where he was a merchant and a justice of the peace. Both his grandfathers were prominent merchants. On the death of his parents, in 1760, John Pintard was adopted by his uncle, Louis Pintard, a New York merchant. He was prepared for college at Hempstead, L. I., and was graduated at the College of New Jersey, 1776. He was deputy commissary for the prisoners in New York city under his uncle, serving until 1781, and in 1782 became a clerk in his uncle's counting-room. He married, November 12, 1784, Eliza, daughter of Col. Abraham and Helena (Kortright) Brasher, of Paramus, N. J. Mr. Pintard engaged in the East India trade on his own account in 1785; was an assistant alderman in 1789-90, and represented the city in the State Assembly in the following year. He established a museum in 1791, in connection with the Tammany Society. He resided in New York city in 1800, and was engaged in the book trade and auction business. In the winter of 1801 he went to New Orleans, La., where he gathered valuable statistics relating to the territory, which contributed to its purchase. He edited the *Daily Advertiser*, 1802; was Clerk to the Corporation of New York city, and City Inspector, 1804-09; secretary of the Mutual Insurance Company, 1809-29, and a director of the same, 1829-44. He was secretary of the New York Chamber of Commerce, 1817-27; he was one of the incorporators of the first savings bank that was established in New York city in 1819, and served as its president, 1828-41, when he became blind, and resigned. He was among the first, in 1805, to agitate the "free school system," and was influential in securing the construction of the Erie Canal. He was secretary, 1816-32, and vice-president, 1832-44, of the American Bible Society; a vestryman of the Huguenot church,

New York city, 1810-14; treasurer of Sailors' Snug Harbor, 1819-23; and one of the benefactors of the General Theological Seminary. Pintard Hall, one of the dormitories of the seminary, was erected in his honor in 1885. He received the degree LL.D. from Allegheny College in 1822.

Mr. Pintard was recording secretary of the Society, 1805-19; librarian, 1810-11; treasurer, 1819-27.

At a meeting held October 12, 1816, the Society adopted the following preamble and resolution:

"*Whereas,* The Historical Society of this State is most materially indebted to Mr. John Pintard for his long-continued, faithful, and important services;

"*Resolved,* That in testimony of their due consideration of the same, Mr. Pintard be requested to sit for his portrait for this Society."

Mr. Pintard's portrait was painted for the Society by Trumbull, in 1817.

Mr. Pintard died June 21, 1844. The Society, at its regular meeting held October 1, 1844, adopted the following resolution:

"*Resolved,* That in the decease of John Pintard, LL.D., this Society has lost one of its earliest and most devoted friends, one of those, indeed, to whom the institution owes its origin, and much of its usefulness.

"*Resolved,* That the memory of Mr. Pintard is cherished by the members of this Society, for the many excellent features of his private and public character."

Federal Hall, the first home of the Society, stood on the northeast corner of Wall and Nassau Streets, erected in 1700 as the second City Hall, succeeding the first City Hall, or Stadt Huys erected in 1642 on Pearl Street.

In 1788 the Common Council resolved to appropriate the whole of the City Hall to the uses of the General Government, and adopted a plan for the alteration of the building.

The First Congress of the United States met in the reconstructed building on March 4, 1789, when on April 30th Washington was inaugurated first President of the United States. The ceremony took place in the open gallery in front of the Senate-chamber, which looked out upon Broad Street. The Society held meetings in this building until 1809. It has in its custody a section of the iron railing of the balcony, also several chairs and desks used by the officers and members of the first Federal Congress.

Unhappily, this historic building, the most suggestive monument of the events which took place within its old walls, already laden with the memories of a century of occupation and use for public purposes, was heedlessly swept away a few years after it had been decorated by its greatest honor. The edifice was taken down in 1812.

An address to the public, setting forth the objects of the institution, together with several queries as to those points on which the Society requested particular information, was printed in the newspapers of the day. The next publication was its constitution and by-laws, contained in a pamphlet of fifteen pages, published in 1805. These subsequently were printed in the first volume of collections of the Society.

On April 13, 1807, the recording secretary stated that he had in his possession a considerable number of books relating to the history of America, which he was willing to dispose of at the original cost; whereupon the following resolution was adopted:

"*Resolved,* That the standing committee be authorized to purchase said books for the use of the Society."

The liberal donations subsequently made, together with other purchases, soon formed a creditable library in the department of American history. The prospects of the Society now began to brighten, numerous resident and honorary members were elected, and the patriotic objects of the institution rendered it deservedly popular. Application was made to the Legislature for an act of incorporation, which was passed February 10, 1809.

At the meeting held January 10, 1809, attention was called to the fact that this year was the beginning of the third century since the discovery of this part of North America by Henry Hudson. It was then

"*Resolved,* That this Society will commemorate this important event, and that the Rev. Dr. Miller, corresponding secretary, be requested to prepare a discourse for the occasion."

A committee was appointed to examine and ascertain the exact date of this discovery, who subsequently reported "that the 'Journal of the Voyage of Henry Hudson,' contained in 'Purchas Pilgrim,' appeared to be the most authentic and satisfactory document on the subject; and that Captain Hudson, who sailed from Holland in the month of March, 1609, discovered and entered the river, since called by his name, on the fourth day of September following."

That day was accordingly designated for the proposed celebration. The use of the front courtroom in Federal Hall was granted to the Society for the occasion, where "the Rev. Dr. Miller delivered a learned and interesting discourse, illustrative of this event, before a large and respectable audience of ladies and gentlemen, among whom were his Excellency the Governor, and the Mayor and Corporation of the city."

After the discourse, in the language of the minutes, "the Society adjourned to the City Hotel, where, together with a number of invited guests, (at four o'clock) they sat down to an elegant dinner prepared by Messrs. Fay and Gibson, consisting of a variety of shell and other fish with which our waters abound, wild pigeon and *succotash,* the favorite dish of the season (Indian corn and beans), with the different meats introduced into this country by the European settlers."

The following commemorative toasts were drank on the occasion:

1. Christopher Columbus, the discoverer of

America. His monument is not inscribed with his name, yet all nations shall recognize it. Its base covers half the globe, and its summit reaches beyond the clouds.

2. Queen Isabella of Spain, the magnanimous and munificent friend and patroness of Columbus.

3. John and Sebastian Cabot, the contemporaries of Columbus, and the discoverers of North America.

4. John Verrazzano. His enterprising genius and his visit about the 20th of April, 1524, to this part of our country deserve to be better known.

5. Henry Hudson, the enterprising and intrepid navigator. Though disastrous his end, yet fortunate is his renown, for the majestic river which bears his name shall render it immortal.

6. The 4th of September, 1609. The day on which Hudson landed on our shores.

7. Wouter Van Twiller, the first Governor of New Netherlands.

8. Peter Stuyvesant, the last Dutch Governor, an intrepid soldier and faithful officer.

9. Richard Nicolls, the first English Governor of the Province of New York.

10. George Clinton, the first Governor of the State of New York.

11. William Smith, the historian of New York.

12. Richard Hakluyt and Samuel Purchas. May future compilers of historical documents emulate their diligence and fidelity.

13. William Stith, Cadwallader Colden, Samuel

Smith, Jeremy Belknap, and George R. Minot, American historians. They have merited the gratitude of their country.

14. The United States of America. May our prosperity ever confirm the belief that the discovery of our country was a blessing to mankind.

15. The State of New York. May it ever be the pleasing task of the historians to record events that shall evince the wisdom of her Legislature and display the virtues of her people.

16. The Massachusetts Historical Society, which set the honorable example of collecting and preserving what relates to the history of our country.

17. Our forefathers, to whose enterprise and fortitude, under Providence, we owe the blessings we enjoy.

Among the volunteer toasts given were the following, after his Excellency the Governor and the Mayor had retired:

By Mr. William Johnson, chairman: The Governor of the State of New York.

By Mr. John Pintard: The Mayor and Corporation of the City of New York.

By Dr. Samuel L. Mitchill: A speedy termination of our foreign relations.

By Col. Jonathan Williams, United States Engineers: May our knowledge of past times teach us to enjoy the present and improve the future.

By Simeon De Witt, Surveyor General: May our successors, a century hence, celebrate the same event which we this day commemorate.

By Dr. David Hosack, Professor of Botany, Columbia College: The memory of St. Nicholas. May the virtuous habits and simple manners of our Dutch ancestors be not lost in the luxuries and refinements of the present times.

By Mr. Nathaniel Pendleton: May the same virtues and the same industry continue in our land which have converted an Indian cornfield into a botanic garden.

By Mr. Anthony Bleecker: The Memory of General Washington.

By Mr. Josiah Ogden Hoffman: Egbert Benson, our absent and respected president.

By Dr. John Bullus, agent United States Navy: The Lieutenant-Governor (John Broome) of the State of New York.

By Dr. Archibald Bruce, Professor of Mineralogy, College of Physicians: The Rev. Dr. Miller. His interesting discourse of to-day affords a pleasing anticipation of his promised history of New York.

By Col. Peter Curtenius, of the New York Artillery: Pierre Van Cortlandt, the first Lieutenant-Governor of the State of New York.

By Mr. Henry Gahn, the Swedish Consul: The Mouth of the Hudson. May it soon have a sharp set of teeth, to show its defense.

By the Recording Secretary: The American Fair, without whose endearing society this western world, the rich inheritance from our enterprising ancestors, would still be a wilderness indeed.

The publication of the first volume of its collections is distinctly due to the enthusiasm produced by this generous banquet. A committee was appointed, after the delivery of the discourse, " to report materials for forming a volume of the proceedings of this Society, together with such tracts relating to the history of this country as may merit republication."

The anniversary meetings of the Society were held on St. Nicholas Day, December 6th. The customary place of dining on these occasions was for several years at Kent's Hotel, 42 Broad Street.

A communication was received from the Academy of Arts, September 9, 1809, inviting the Society to occupy a room in the Government House. The invitation was promptly accepted, and on September 15th the first meeting was held there. The northwest room in the second story of that building was appropriated to the use of the Society. The books, which had been previously kept in the City Library, were removed to the same place.

The Government House, at the foot of Broadway, facing Bowling Green, stood on the site of Fort Amsterdam, which after the conquest was called Fort James, in compliment to the Duke of York; in the reign of William and Mary, Fort William; and in the following reigns, Fort Anne and Fort George. The Government House was originally designed for the residence of Washington, then President of the United States, but as the capital removed to Philadelphia, the house was never occupied by him. It then became the Government House, and was the residence of Governor George Clinton and John Jay, and from 1799 to 1815 used for the Custom-House, when it was taken down and succeeded by a handsome block of houses. The new Custom-House is now in course of erection on this site.

In March, 1810, a petition of the Society, signed by Egbert Benson, president, praying that the Legislature would grant them such aid as they should deem meet and the general interest of the State would permit, to accomplish the objects for which the Society was associated and incorporated, was presented to the Legislature of New York. The following letters from De Witt Clinton and Dr. Mitchell, members of the Senate and Assembly respectively, show the action of that body:

ALBANY, *March 22*, 1810.

DEAR SIR: I have the pleasure of informing you that the bill for endowing the Historical Society, and killing the wolves and panthers, passed the the Senate this morning without opposition. If the Federal Assembly shall act as liberally as the Republican Senate, it will go down, but I am fearful that your party will be very deficient in this respect.

The Mechanics' Bank bill has passed the Senate with equal unanimity.

I am, dear sir, yours sincerely,

DE WITT CLINTON.

JOHN PINTARD, Esq.

ALBANY, *April* 3, 1810.

DEAR SIR: I have the mortification to inform you that the bill from the Senate for the destruction of wild beasts, and for the encouragement of history, was this day debated and finally rejected. The vote, in spite of all that the friends of the projects could say, was 43 to 27. I supported it with as good a speech as I could make. But all was in vain. The great objection was that too many lottery jobs had been authorized already, and under this influence the thing would not work. Van Horne made the motion to reject. He ought to be conveyed to his native town in a car drawn by wolves, panthers, and wild-cats.

The public business has rendered it necessary to prolong the session from the 2d instant, as originally agreed upon for the adjournment to Thursday, the 5th. On Saturday I hope to move homeward in the steamboat.

Truly yours, as ever,

S. L. MITCHILL.

John Pintard, in a letter dated August 28, 1812, addressed to the Hon. De Witt Clinton, Mayor of the City of New York, formulated a plan to combine in one building, if possible, with the patronage of the city, the Academy of Arts, City Library, Historical Society, and the American Museum, with some other institutions that ought to be established and promoted, with all that at present exists in this city relating to these subjects, and that by concentrating all our resources we may give a greater impulse and elevation to our intellectual character, and suggested that either the Almshouse, or Bridewell, in the Park, would be suitable buildings for the purpose.

This letter has the following endorsement:

"Memo. Mr. Clinton, on reading this communication, observed 'that the request was too impudent to be submitted to the Corporation!'"

"Never Despair" was the motto used by Mr. Pintard on his book-plate.

He did not despair, for on December 7th of the same year the Society, in conjunction with the New York Society Library and the Academy of Arts, petitioned the Corporation of the city for the use of the Almshouse, or the Bridewell, for the use of the above institutions, and other scientific institutions to be established in this city. Three years later the city authorities set apart the Almshouse for the use of the several institutions, the name of the building being changed to the New York Institution.

The Rev. Dr. Timothy Alden (later President of Meadville College, Pa.), happening to be on a visit to this city, January 11, 1813, offered his services for the preparation of a catalogue, which the Society accepted. The catalogue was printed December 22, 1813, at first separately, and subsequently in the second volume of the collections of the Society.

The catalogue shows that the library consisted at that time of 4,265 titles of books and pamphlets;

234 volumes of United States documents; 130 titles of American newspapers; 134 maps and charts; 30 miscellaneous views; 119 almanacs; a portion of "Sterling Papers," with 48 separate manuscripts; 16 manuscript volumes of the House of Commons, 1650-76; several portraits in oil, and 38 engraved portraits—quite a collection brought together in the nine years of the existence of the Society.

On January 11, 1814, it was "*Resolved,* that application be made to the Legislature of this State for their patronage of this Society, and that Mr. Clinton be appointed to draft a suitable memorial on the subject."

At the next quarterly meeting, held April 12th, Mr. Clinton informed the Society that, agreeably to their request at the last meeting, he had drawn up a memorial to the Legislature of this State for their patronage, which he presented at the present sessions of both Houses. That a clause granting this Society $12,000, which was included in the bill, entitled "An Act for instituting a Lottery for the promotion of Literature," had passed the Senate, but was non-concurred in in the House of Assembly. Ayes, 41; nays, 44.

This act became a law on April 15, 1814. The following is an abstract of the same:

"Section 51. *And be it further enacted,* That the managers to be appointed in compliance with the act, entitled 'An Act instituting a Lottery for the promotion of Literature, and for other purposes,' after the payments are completed, according to the several provisions contained in said act, be and hereby are directed to raise the additional sum of twelve thousand dollars in the manner directed in and by the aforesaid act, which sum, when so raised, shall be paid to the Historical Society in the city of New York, for the purpose of procuring books, manuscripts, and other materials, to illustrate the natural, literary, civil, and ecclesiastical history of America."

The Society unfortunately engaged its credit in the purchase of books and of manuscripts before it was known how distant and precarious were the proceeds of this mode of raising money. It thus became involved in a debt which was not extinguished without many and severe sacrifices. It had, however, before its usefulness was impeded by the pressure of this debt, published several volumes of transactions of great value.

The debt incurred by the Society in anticipation of the funds to be received from this lottery amounted to several thousand dollars, and was chiefly assumed by the librarian, Dr. John W. Francis, to whom a mortgage on the property of the Society was executed by way of security. At length, after a long-continued struggle with pecuniary embarrassments and difficulties, an arrangement was entered into with Union College, by which the Society agreed to take eight thousand dollars in cash for its lottery interest, out of which sum, in 1823, the debts were paid.

Many valuable additions were made during the time that Dr. Francis officiated as librarian. Among the original papers, the military correspondence of Gen. Horatio Gates was secured, July, 1816, through the influence of the celebrated Robert Fulton, then a resident member of the Society. The papers had been bequeathed by General Gates to Joel Barlow, who contemplated writing a history of the Revolution; but on the death of Barlow, in Europe, his widow had been induced by Mr. Fulton to transfer them to the Society.

A special meeting of the Society was called August 13, 1814, in consequence of the exposed situation of this city to invasion by the enemy, and the danger attending a state of siege and possible bombardment.

The Society, taking the matter into serious consideration,

"*Resolved,* That the library of this Society be packed up in suitable boxes, ready to be removed and sent to some secure place up the Hudson River in case of necessity, and that Dr. Mitchill, Dr. Francis, and the Rev. Mr. Alden be a committee to carry this resolution into effect."

On January 14, 1815, Dr. Francis reported "that, in conformity with the resolution passed at the last meeting of the Society, the committee had caused all the most valuable and scarce books in the library to be carefully packed in portable cases. But that, happily, the campaign of 1814 had passed by without a necessity for removing them from the dangers of an hostile attack on this city. As, however, a similar cause may exist should the war between the United States and Great Britain

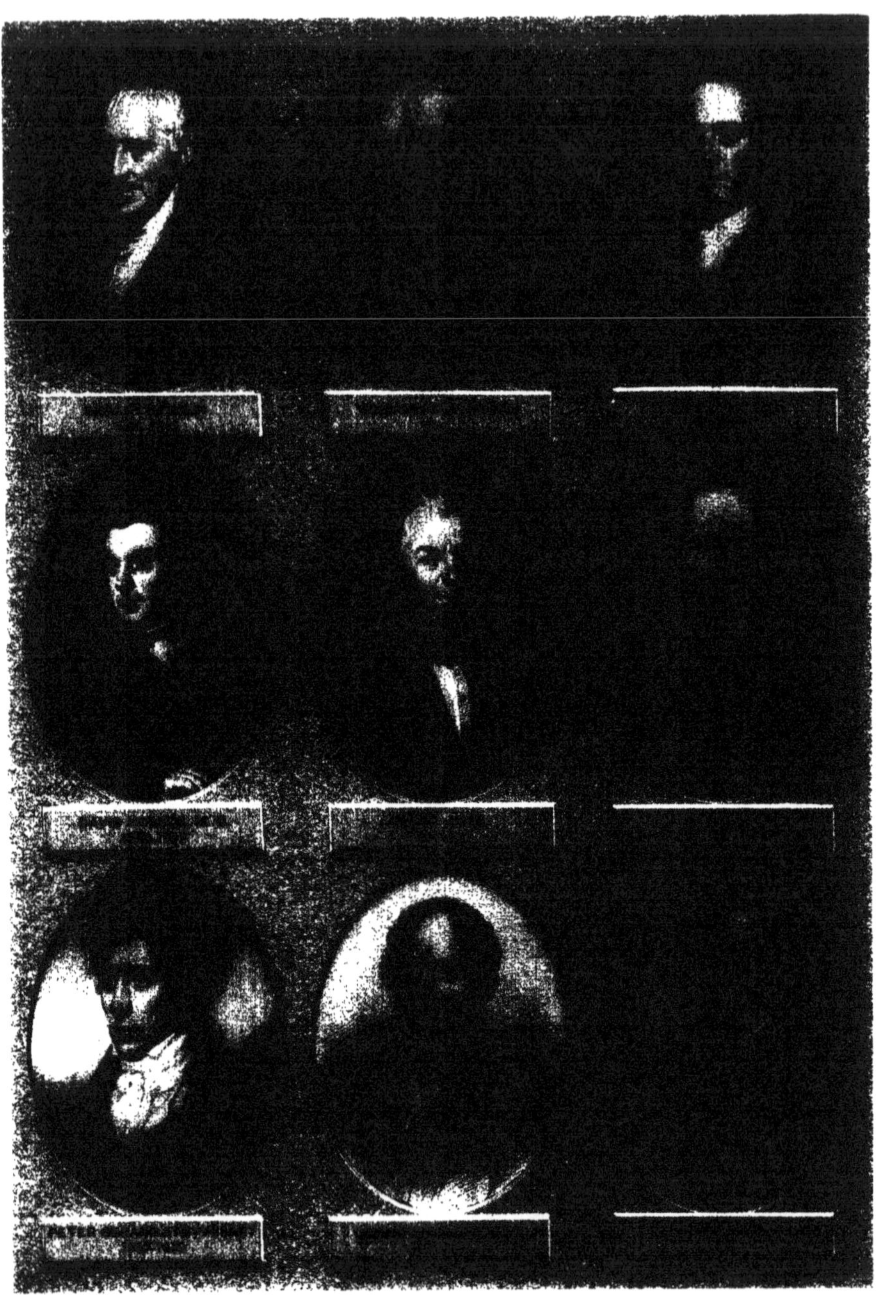

PRESIDENTS

continue, it was recommended to leave the books packed up ready for removal in case of emergency."

On June 15, 1815, Mr. Pintard reported that "the Corporation of the city, on May 22d last, had appropriated the Almshouse, in rear of the City Hall, when no longer required for public use, to the several literary and scientific societies which had petitioned for their patronage. That the new almshouse established at Bellevue would be completed for the reception of the tenants of the present almshouse in the course of this year.

"And, further, that as the Corporation had resolved to sell the Government House and ground thereto belonging, the fee-simple of which had been purchased from the State, it is necessary to remove the library of the Society to some place until possession can be obtained of the apartments to be allotted to the Society in the New York Institution, formerly the Almshouse. The library of the Society was temporarily stored in the store of Capt. James Farquhar, in Vesey Street, together with the pictures, casts, busts, etc., belonging to the Academy of Arts, until their removal in 1816 to the New York Institution."

The Hon. Gouverneur Morris, who had been vice-president, 1810-15, was elected president of the Society, at the annual meeting held January 9, 1816.

At a meeting held July 30, 1816, the following resolution was adopted:

"*Resolved,* That the Society commemorate the

discovery of this part of the Continent of North America by Hudson in 1609, on Wednesday, the fourth day of September next, being the 207th anniversary of this memorable event. And that the inauguration of the Hon. Gouverneur Morris, president-elect of this Society, take place on that day, at twelve o'clock, and that suitable accommodations be provided for the ladies who may honor the Society with their presence on that occasion."

Through the courtesy of Mayor Radcliff the Society assembled at eleven o'clock on September 4th in the Sessions Court-Room in the City Hall, where the formal inauguration of Mr. Morris as president of the Society took place.

Gouverneur Morris, statesman and orator, was born in Morrisania, January 31, 1752; died there, November 6, 1816; graduate of Kings College (now Columbia), 1768; member of Continental Congress, 1777-80; United States Minister to France, 1792-94; he succeeded in 1810 the Hon. Brockholst Livingston as vice-president of the Society.

The Society, on November 12, 1816, adopted the following resolution on the death of Mr. Morris:

"*Resolved,* That, as a tribute of respect to the memory of the Hon. Gouverneur Morris, deceased, late president of the Society, the members wear the accustomed badge of mourning for thirty days."

The Society met for the first time in the New

York Institution, late Almshouse, July 9, 1816, occupying two rooms adjoining each other, on the first floor, on the southerly side of the building, and on the easterly side of the middle entry, with same accommodation in the basement. The premises were leased to the Society by the Corporation of the city for a term of ten years dating from April 1, 1815, at a yearly rent of one peppercorn, "if lawfully demanded." The other occupants of the building were the Literary and Philosophical Society, the American Academy of Fine Arts, the Lyceum of Natural History, and Scudder's American Museum. The edifice was erected in 1795, and was 260 feet long by 44 broad, with two projections in front, 15 by 20 feet each, and was composed of brick, three stories high, with a basement, and with no claim to beauty.

Owing to the fact that the New York Society Library had decided not to occupy rooms allotted to them in the New York Institution, by the Corporation of the city, the Historical Society requested from the Corporation of the city these additional rooms, for the establishment of a mineralogical cabinet and other purposes. This request was granted, and two southerly rooms on the west side of the middle entry, opposite to the rooms already occupied by them, were set apart. It was made a condition that the Society also accommodate the American Bible Society with the use of a room for their meetings.

Dr. Mitchill, De Witt Clinton, and Col. George Gibbs were among the most zealous amateurs of natural science. Col. Gibbs, who was chairman of the mineralogical committee, was particularly active in promoting the collection of minerals and specimens of natural history. A series of lectures was established February 11, 1817, on zoölogy, geology, vegetable physiology, mineralogy, chemistry, and philosophy. The growth of this department became so large, and predominated over the real purposes of the Society to such an extent that in 1829 it was decided to present the collection to the Lyceum of Natural History, organized February 24, 1817, for the exclusive pursuit of those branches of science.

The Hon. De Witt Clinton, vice-president of the Society, 1810-16, succeeded the late Gouverneur Morris as third president of the Society, January 14, 1817.

The Chamber of Commerce of New York, at a meeting held November 7, 1769, had requested its president to ask David Rittenhouse and Capt. John Montressor to take the latitude of the southwest bastion of Fort George. At a meeting of this Society, held June 10, 1817, an abstract of these minutes of the Chamber was read by Mr. Pintard (then secretary of the Chamber). On motion, John Pintard, Dr. John Griscom, and Dr. Samuel L. Mitchill were appointed a committee to prepare a memorial to the Common Council, for the erection of a monument to mark the site. The Common Council reported in favor of the Society's memorial, and in the following year erected a block of white marble, properly inscribed, on the site of the southwest bastion. On July 30, 1905, this relic was unearthed by laborers in the subway excavation in Battery Park. The Society has secured the custody of the monument, with a view to its re-erection in the near future. The original inscription for the monument, as proposed in 1817, is in the archives of the Society.

An extensive and valuable cabinet of coins and medals was presented to the Society, July 14, 1818, by the heirs of Rev. Dr. John C. Kunze, pastor of the Lutheran Church in Frankfort Street, 1784-1807. This collection was stolen from the Society a few years after its reception, nothing remaining but the cabinet which held the coins and medals.

Dr. David Hosack, corresponding secretary, 1814-16, and vice-president, 1817-18, became the fourth president on the retirement of De Witt Clinton, January 11, 1820. He was one of the eleven who met to organize the Society, November 20, 1804.

Owing to the prevalence of yellow fever, no meetings of the Society were held during the months of August, September, and October, 1822.

General Lafayette and his son, George Washington Lafayette, were elected honorary members, August 18, 1824, and at a special meeting held the following day a reception was tendered to these gentlemen. Addresses were made by the president, Dr. Hosack, and General Lafayette. The Society has two portraits of Lafayette, one painted in France, and presented to the Society by Gen. Ebenezer Stevens, October 7, 1817. Also the portrait painted from life in 1825, by Ingham, and is the original head from which was made the full-length portrait for the State, presented to the Society by the artist.

A communication was read at the meeting December 14, 1824, from James Renwick and William Gracie, a committee appointed by the Associates of the New York Athenæum for the purpose of conferring with the Historical Society, the Society Library, and the Trustees of Columbia College on the subject of a union of their several interests (in such a way as to form one great public library), requesting this matter to be brought before the Society with the view to the appointment of a committee of conference in its behalf. A committee was appointed, consisting of Dr. Hosack, chairman, and Anthony Bleecker and Colonel Stone.

At a meeting held February 8, 1825, Mr. Bleecker informed the Society that "the abovementioned committee had met the committee of the other institutions, and that a project is contemplated to be laid before the several institutions for the purpose of effecting this union." This attempt of consolidation of the various institutions was not successful.

Notwithstanding the liberal grant of the Legislature, the Society became again seriously embarrassed by debt, and so desperate was its condition regarded, that at a meeting held April 12, 1825, on motion of Dr. De Kay, seconded by the Rev. Mr. Jones, it was

"*Resolved,* That it is expedient that a committee

of members be appointed to endeavor to extricate this Society from its present embarrassments, with full powers to bargain, sell, and convey (either in whole or in part, as circumstances may require) the property belonging to the Society (except donations), and to use any other means which they may deem proper for the obtaining of that object."

At a special meeting held on Saturday, April 16, to take action on the above resolution, the following committee was appointed: Dr. De Kay, Rev. Cave Jones, Anthony Bleecker, William Gracie, Benjamin Haight.

The committee reported, May 28, that the whole debt of the Society amounted to $7,500. To pay off this debt, the committee made arrangements for the sale, in whole or in part, of the library. Many offers were received, among them one from Mr. Isaac S. Hone, making an offer to purchase the library, with the intention of presenting it to the New York Athenæum.

This offer led to serious results. The committee did not consider they had authority to sell the whole library, and therefore called a meeting of the Society to obtain further power.

A resolution ordering the sale of the property of the Society was adopted at the June 14, 1825, meeting by a vote of ten to six. Previous to the question being taken on the resolution, Dr. Hosack, the president, tendered his resignation, and Colonel Trumbull took the chair. After the question on the resolution was acted on, Colonel Trumbull also tendered his resignation of the office of second vice-president, and, together with Dr. Hosack, withdrew. Dr. De Kay and Mr. Gracie resigned as members of the committee; Mr. Frederic de Peyster and Mr. Joseph Blunt were appointed to the vacancies. This was the last meeting of the Society until March 14, 1826, when, according to the minutes, Dr. Hosack presided, and Colonel Trumbull was recorded as present as vice-president. Evidently the Society had taken no action on the resignations of these gentlemen as president and vice-president.

On January 13, 1827, a memorial setting forth the financial difficulties of the Society was submitted, and Mr. Frederic de Peyster was requested to present it at Albany. Mr. de Peyster accordingly repaired to Albany during the session of 1827, and, with the aid of Governor Clinton, succeeded in obtaining a grant of five thousand dollars, on condition that the debts of the Society should be so reduced as to render that sum sufficient to liquidate them altogether. This liberal donation was received in April, 1828, and, upon the nomination of Mr. de Peyster, the members of that Legislature were elected honorary members of the Society.

Another attempt to house all the literary and scientific societies in the city in one building was made at a public meeting held in the Common Council Chamber, May 17, 1827.

It was proposed to apply to the Corporation of the city for a lease for ninety-nine years of the building known as the New York Institution, City

Hall Park, to be appropriated for the accommodation of the New York Historical Society, the New York Horticultural Society, the Literary and Philosophical Society, the American Academy of Fine Arts, the New York Lyceum, the New York Athenæum, the New York Society Library, and the Law Library Association.

This plan was abandoned, the anticipated aid not having been obtained, and small encouragement being held out to those directly interested in the measure suggested for carrying out fully and appropriately a design so important to the various institutions throughout the city and to the public at large.

On January 15, 1828, the Hon. James Kent, LL.D., succeeded Dr. Hosack as the fifth president of the Society.

James Kent, jurist, was born in Doanesburgh, N. Y., July 31, 1763; died in this city, December 12, 1847; graduated at Yale College, 1781; studied law with Egbert Benson; admitted to the bar, 1785; member of Assembly, 1791-93 and 1796; Professor of Law in Columbia College, 1793; Recorder of this city, 1797; Judge of Supreme Court, 1798; Chief Justice, July, 1804; and Chancellor, 1814-23; author of "Commentaries on the United States Constitution," and a treatise on the city charter and the powers of the municipal officers. He was not only an eminent jurist, but was one of the first legal writers of his time. His anniversary address before the Society, December 6, 1828, was published in 1829.

Three volumes of collections had already been published; a fourth was added in 1828, containing a continuation of Smith's "History of New York" to the year 1762, from the original manuscript of the author, presented for the purpose by his son, William Smith, of Quebec. The first volume, extending to 1732, was printed in London in 1757. The Society, in 1829, reprinted both volumes in a uniform edition, under the supervision of Dr. Francis, John Delafield, and Dr. Hosack. A memoir of the author, written by his son, was prefixed to this edition.

The publications of the Society at this period were numerous. Among them may be mentioned the catalogue of the library, memorials to the Legislature with accompanying documents, Dr. Hosack's memoir of Hugh Williamson, delivered before the Society, and the annual addresses of Chancellor Kent, William Sampson, Joseph Blunt, and William Beach Lawrence. The discourse of the venerable Egbert Benson, the first president of the Society, delivered in 1816, was printed at his own expense. This circumstance arose from objections having been made to certain portions of the discourse by individuals who were desirous they should be omitted if published by the Society. At these suggestions Judge Benson took offence, as appears from some remarks relating to the subject published with the memoir. He printed a new edition, with copious notes, in 1825, at Jamaica, Long Island. Judge Benson's discourse is a remarkable production, both as to matter and style.

It professedly treats of local names in this State, whether of Indian or European origin.

In 1829 the Corporation of the city notified the Society that the rooms occupied by them were needed for the use of the city. Notwithstanding this notice, the Society received an extension of time, and did not remove until three years later.

At the annual meeting, January 10, 1832, the Hon. Morgan Lewis was elected the sixth president of the Society.

Morgan Lewis, son of Francis Lewis, signer of the Declaration of Independence, born in New York, October 16, 1754; died there, April 7, 1844; graduate of the College of New Jersey, 1773; He studied law in the office of John Jay; was Major of the Second Regiment New York City Militia, Col. John Jay, November 3, 1775; Colonel and Deputy Quartermaster-General in the Northern Department of the Continental Army, September 12, 1776, to the close of the war of the American Revolution. Admitted to the bar after the war, he practised in Dutchess County; member of Assembly 1789-90 and 1792; Attorney-General of the State, 1791; Judge of Supreme Court, 1792; Chief Justice in 1801; Governor of the State, 1804-07, State Senator 1811-14; Major-General in the War of 1812.

In this year the Society received its first legacy, amounting to $300, a bequest of Isaiah Thomas, journalist and author, and founder of the American Antiquarian Society of Worcester, Mass., who died April 4, 1831. The principal is still held intact, and is known as the "Isaiah Thomas Fund."

Having occupied rooms in the New York Institution sixteen years by a gratuitous lease from the city, on April 19, 1832, the Society took possession of the third floor of the new building erected by Peter Remsen, and known as the Remsen Building, at the southwest corner of Broadway and Chambers Street. On this occasion a discourse was delivered by William Beach Lawrence. This change of location proved unfavorable to the interests of the Society. The rent of the hall, and other expenditures, led to the creation of a new debt. The treasurer, John Delafield, generously assumed full responsibility for the amount.

During the period July, 1833, to December, 1835, inclusive, no minutes of the meetings are preserved.

Peter Gerard Stuyvesant was elected the seventh president of the Society, at an annual meeting held in the Remsen Building, January 3, 1836. Mr. Stuyvesant was the great-great-grandson of Governor Petrus Stuyvesant; was born in 1778; died August 16, 1847. Mr. Stuyvesant was one of the original eleven who met on November 20, 1804, to organize the Society.

Measures were now taken for relieving the Society from its embarrassments. The treasurer was authorized to raise one thousand dollars on the credit of the institution, and a committee was appointed to select a new location. Several offers were made at this period, by different public institutions, for the gratuitous accommodation of the Society; among them was the Stuyvesant Institute, an association for literary purposes, by whom a building had been erected at 659 Broadway, opposite Bond Street, September 1, 1837. The offer was accepted. In the summer of 1837 the Society removed to its new quarters, with a generous lease of two spacious rooms for the term of ten years.

Active measures were now taken to restore the prosperity of the Society. A public course of historical lectures was determined upon, which was commenced in January, 1838, by a brilliant discourse by the Rev. Dr. Francis L. Hawks, before a crowded assemblage in the spacious lecture-room of the Stuyvesant Institute. This was followed by a series of lectures, chiefly from members of the Society, which was fully attended. The pecuniary proceeds of this course of lectures sufficed to extinguish the debts of the Society.

At the meeting held April 10, 1838, a resolution was adopted by the Society to memorialize the Legislature on the subject of collecting materials in Europe illustrative of the history of New York. The memorial was approved at the meeting held January 8, 1839, presented to the Legislature the same month, and forwarded to that body by a special message from Governor Seward on February 5th following. It was adopted with great unanimity. John Romeyn Brodhead was appointed by the Governor and Senate the agent of the State under the act passed. As a result of his labors abroad, the State has published ten large folio volumes and index, of the highest importance not only to the student, but to the public at large. Besides this attention to the views of the Society, the Legislature, in compliance with another recommendation, ordered the publication of the journals of the New York Provincial Congress and Convention, together with the proceedings of the Committee of Safety, from May, 1775, to the adoption of the State Constitution.

The semi-centennial anniversary of the first inauguration of George Washington was celebrated by the Society, April 30, 1839. The Hon. John Quincy Adams, the sixth President of the United States, was selected as the orator. Mr. Adams arrived in town from Washington on Monday, April 29th, and in the evening met a large number of the members of the Society at its rooms. From thence the company repaired by invitation to the residence of Mr. Stuyvesant, president of the Society, where a sumptuous entertainment was provided for the occasion.

On Tuesday, at eleven o'clock A.M., the Society with their guests assembled at the City Hotel, where a large number of citizens joined them in paying their personal respects to the venerable orator of the day, and to the Revolutionary veterans, who, disregarding the infirmities of age, had once more rallied in honor of their beloved chief.

At twelve o'clock the company moved in procession to the Middle Dutch Church, where an immense concourse of people was assembled. A temporary stage was erected in front of the pulpit for the convenience of the guests. Peter G. Stuyvesant presided. The exercises were opened by prayer by the Rev. Dr. John Knox, associate pastor of the Collegiate Dutch Church, followed by an ode written for the occasion by William Cullen Bryant.

The address of Mr. Adams, entitled "The Jubilee of the Constitution," by the extraordinary ability, learning, and eloquence which it displayed, fully sustained the most sanguine anticipations of the friends of the distinguished orator. The exercises were concluded with a prayer and benediction by the Rev. Dr. Jonathan M. Wainwright, of Trinity Church.

At six o'clock P.M. the company reassembled at the City Hotel, and about two hundred persons sat down to a dinner prepared in the best style of that well-known establishment. Thirteen regular and twenty-one volunteer toasts were tendered, and two odes by Grenville Mellen and William Cutter were read by the authors.

In the course of the evening a fine transparency representing old Federal Hall, formerly standing on the corner of Wall and Nassau Streets, the scene of Washington's inauguration, was disclosed by the withdrawal of a curtain at the upper end of the hall, and produced a brilliant effect. The figures of Washington and Chancellor Livingston were seen in the balcony, the one laying his hand upon the book, while the other administered the oath of office.

On the approach of the centennial of the same

event, the Executive Committee was directed to formulate a plan for a suitable celebration of the occasion. This action on the part of the Society was followed by similar action on the part of the Chamber of Commerce and the Society of the Sons of the Revolution. The final result was the appointment of a citizens' committee, who took charge of the whole affair.

Peter Augustus Jay, LL.D., succeeded Mr. Stuyvesant, as the eighth president of the Society, January 14, 1840. Mr. Jay was born in Elizabethtown, N. J., January 24, 1776, and was the eldest son of John Jay, the statesman. He was graduated from Columbia College in 1794, and accompanied his father to England, acting as his private secretary. On his return to New York he studied law, attaining great distinction soon after his admission to the bar. He was a member of the State Assembly in 1816; Recorder of New York, 1819-20. He presented to the Society many books and publications of the colonial period. Mr. Jay died in this city February 20, 1843.

The Society was again forced to move, in consequence of the sale of the Stuyvesant Institute under a foreclosure of a mortgage. In this emergency Mr. Peter G. Stuyvesant offered to convey to the Society two lots of ground fronting on Stuyvesant Street, 40 by 70 feet, on condition that the lots be held in perpetuity by the Society, and that the amount of $18,000 be raised by the Society on or before May 1, 1841, for the erection of a building on the site offered. It was deemed inexpedient, however, to attempt to raise the amount of money required for this object.

In the meantime a liberal proposal from the New York University was accepted. On April 6, 1841, the Committee on New Location reported that accommodations could be obtained in the New York University on the following terms.

" The library to be placed in the room occupied by the University library, second floor above the basement and on the same floor with the chapel. The standard books of the University to remain in a case to be provided by the University.

The gallery above to contain the cabinet and museum of the Historical Society and of the University, and such books and pamphlets as the two librarians might think proper.

All books of each library to be open to the University and the Historical Society, under regulations to be adopted by the librarians, under the advice of their several committees.

The expense of placing the library in the building to be borne by the Society. The expense of lighting, fuel, servants' hire, etc., to be equally divided between the University and the Society.

The salary of the assistant librarian, including any charges for necessary assistance, to be equally divided; and in the settlement of the yearly account for such expenses, one hundred dollars to be allowed to the University.

The large or the small chapel to be used for lectures by the Society on the most liberal terms which the University could afford to any association or individual."

The Society, on May 22, 1841, accepted the liberal offer of the New York University, and a committee was appointed to complete the arrangements.

On October 5th following the Society held its first meeting in the rooms of the University. At this meeting a communication from the Secretary of the Board of Trustees of the New York Society Library, dated May 12, 1841, was read, enclosing the following resolutions of that body:

"*Resolved,* That it appears inexpedient to this Board to make arrangements with the Historical Society according to the terms contained in the report of the committee, submitted to this Board on the 19th of April last.

"*Resolved,* That this Board would have no objection to a union of the New York Society Library with the Historical Society, upon such terms of equality as would best promote the interests of both institutions and the cause of literature.

"It having been suggested that the Historical Society may speedily require different apartments from those which they now occupy,

"*Resolved,* That the use of one of the basement stores be tendered to the Historical Society for the deposit of their property until they can obtain suitable accommodations."

A vote of thanks was tendered to the New York Society Library for their offer of the use of their basement store, and the offer was respectfully declined.

At the annual meeting of the Society for the election of officers, January 3, 1843, it was announced that the Hon. Peter Augustus Jay declined a reëlection to the office of President. The vacancy was filled by the election of the Hon. Albert Gallatin, LL.D., as the ninth president.

Mr. Gallatin was born in Geneva, Switzerland, January 29, 1761, and died at Astoria, L. I., August 12, 1849. He was a member of the Pennsylvania State Convention of 1789, and of the Legislature, 1790-92; member of Congress, 1795-1801; Secretary of the United States Treasury, 1801-13; Commissioner to St. Petersburg, 1813; Commissioner to Ghent, where the treaty of peace was made, December 24, 1814; Minister to France, 1815-23; Envoy Extraordinary to Great Britain, 1826-27; President of the Council of the New York University, 1830; President of the New York National Bank, 1831-39; a founder and first president of the Ethnological Society, 1848; author of several works on the Indians and finance.

The fortieth anniversary of the Society was celebrated on November 20, 1844, by an address by John Romeyn Brodhead, delivered at six o'clock in the evening in the Church of the Messiah, Broadway, opposite the then newly erected New York Hotel. After the address the members and guests adjourned to the New York Hotel for dinner.

The Society continued to advance in prosperity and usefulness; its membership was largely increased; the library was much enhanced by valuable additions; the stated meetings were fully attended, and a lively spirit of devotion to the cause for which they associated themselves was shown in the interest of the members generally.

On June 1, 1847, a committee of nine was appointed to solicit subscriptions to raise the sum of $50,000, to be applied to the erection of a permanent fireproof building, the subscriptions to be binding when the sum of $10,000 was subscribed.

It was resolved, on December 19, 1848, to prepare a memorial to the Legislature for an appropriation toward the erection of the proposed new building. The memorial failed to receive the favorable action of the Assembly, thirteen months later.

On Sunday morning, February 3, 1849, the smaller chapel in the University Building, the floor below the rooms of the Society, was discovered to be on fire. The prompt exertions of the inmates of the building, and of the firemen who assembled as soon as the alarm was given, saved the library and collections of the Society. During the excitement caused by the fire, the president's chair was thrown from the window and broken. This chair was purchased by Mr. Gouverneur Morris when Minister to France, at a sale of the contents of the Versailles. It was part of the furniture of Marie Antoinette, and was presented to the

Society, May 6, 1817, by Mrs. Gouverneur Morris, to be used by the presiding officer.

A memorial of the Society was presented to the Corporation of the city, urging the importance of the publication of the minutes of the Common Council. A communication from the latter body was read at the meeting held April 3, 1849, stating that it was inexpedient to comply with the memorial of the Society to print the unpublished proceedings of the Common Council. After a lapse of fifty-five years, the English period of these records (1675-1776) is now in press, under the supervision of a committee of the Society, appointed in response to a second memorial addressed to the Mayor of the city, dated April 1, 1902.

The Hon. Luther Bradish, LL.D., first vice-president since 1845, and who was very active in the advancement of the Society, succeeded the late Albert Gallatin, as the tenth president of the Society, January 2, 1850.

Mr. Bradish was born at Cummington, Mass., September 15, 1783; died at Newport, R. I., August 30, 1863. In 1826 he settled in Franklin County, N. Y., where he was a large land-owner; was member of the Assembly, 1828-30 and 1836-38; Lieutenant-Governor of the State, 1839-43; Assistant United States Treasurer at New York, 1851-52; and at his death was president of this Society and of the American Bible Society.

In 1851 the Society again memorialized the Legislature for aid in the erection of a fireproof building. The Legislature adjourned without taking any action. Four years later the committee on memorializing the Legislature was discharged.

Owing to the insufficiency of accommodations in the library, the place of meetings was changed to the small chapel of the University, on May 4, 1852.

On January 4, 1853, the committee reported that paid subscriptions amounting to $34,920.40 had been received.

In the meantime the following sites for the new building were offered for consideration: Lafayette Place, west side, between Astor Place and Fourth Street; Sixteenth Street near Sixth Avenue, site of the present Everett House, East Seventeenth Street; southwest corner of Broadway and Twentieth Street, and the gore of land, Broadway, Fifth Avenue, Twenty-second to Twenty-third Streets, now occupied by the Fuller Building, known as the "Flatiron."

The Society, by resolution, recommended to the favorable consideration of the Building Committee a site on Second Avenue and Eleventh Street, consisting of 55 feet on Second Avenue by 100 feet on Eleventh Street, with 4½ feet in width adjacent on the avenue, for air and light.

The semi-centennial celebration of the founding of the Society was held at Niblo's Saloon, November 20, 1854, at 2.30 P.M. George Bancroft delivered the address, entitled "The Necessity, the Reality, and the Promise of the Progress of the Human Race."

HOMES OF THE SOCIETY

NEW BUILDING

Seventy-sixth — Seventy-seventh Streets — Central Park West

After the exercises, the Society, with their guests, proceeded to the Astor House, where they sat down to dinner at six o'clock. Thirteen regular and twelve volunteer toasts were offered. The assembly adjourned shortly after twelve o'clock.

The corner-stone of the present building was laid Wednesday, October 17, 1855, by the president of the Society, the Hon. Luther Bradish, with addresses by Frederic de Peyster, Rev. Dr. Bethune, and others. The newspapers of the day report that the stone was so large that fears were entertained that it would break down the platform, but by the aid of a derrick it was placed in position.

After overcoming many serious and almost fatal obstacles to its progress, the Society held its first meeting with dedicatory ceremonies in the present edifice, November 3, 1857; and two weeks later celebrated the fifty-third anniversary of the founding of the institution.

At the first meeing held in its new home, Mr. Benjamin R. Winthrop presented the "Washington Chair" for the use of the presiding officer of the Society. This chair was made of timber from the house occupied by President Washington in 1789, which stood at the junction of Pearl and Cherry Streets, formerly known as St. George's Square, now Franklin Square. The edifice was erected in 1770, for Walter Franklin, a well-known and highly respected citizen. The chair is of oak, neatly carved; the high back is ornamented with scroll-work, in which are appropriately wrought the initials G. W. A bust of Washington, in a wreath of laurel, forms the centre ornament of the upper part of the chair. The front of the seat bears the escutcheon and arms of the United States, while the arms of the city and State of New York are carved in relief on medallions. Mr. Winthrop, seven years later, presented similar chairs for the use of the first and second vice-presidents.

A fund was established by the Society in 1858, for the publication of its transactions and collections in American history. Of the shares of the capital stock of this fund, limited in number to one thousand, 829 have been sold. The interest of the principal is used for the publication of each successive volume. The price of the remaining 171 shares is one hundred dollars per share. Each share is transferrable on the books of the fund, and entitles the holder, his heirs, administrators or assigns to receive all the publications. Thirty volumes have been published as Collections.

The Society had acquired a small collection of portraits, and proposed to enlarge and extend their Art Collections, with a view of providing a public gallery of art in this city.

The entire collection of the New York Gallery of Fine Arts was transferred to the Society in 1858. Any notice of this collection would be deficient which should fail to commemorate the name of Luman Reed, whose taste, judgment, and generosity formed the nucleus of what may now be justly regarded as the foundation of a gallery of art. In this connection the Society was chiefly indebted to the liberality and cordial coöperation of one of their valued members, Mr. Jonathan Sturges, who was the chief promoter of the original design of the New York Gallery of the Fine Arts.

Mr. James Lenox, having acquired the Nineveh Sculptures, presented them to the Society April 5, 1859.

The Abbott Collection of Egyptian Antiquities, collected by Dr. Henry Abbott during a residence of twenty years in Cairo, became the property of the Society through some public-spirited citizens of this city in 1860. The jewelry in the collection is unique, and contains, among other articles, the gold necklace and ear-rings bearing the name of Menes, the first Pharaoh of Egypt; also the large gold signet-ring of Shoufou, or Cheops, as High Priest and King. The collection also contains three large mummies of the Sacred Bull, Apis, the only specimens known in the world.

The Society was the first to formulate a plan to establish a museum and art gallery for the public in Central Park, as may be seen by the action of the Executive Committee, August 14, 1860:

"*Whereas,* The position and character of the building known as the New York State Arsenal, near the southeastern corner of Central Park, point it out as a proper location for a grand museum of antiquities, science, and art;

"And, *Whereas,* There appears to be no existing institution whose present collections and prospects for future acquisitions seem more suitable to the occasion than this Society, the recent and prospective increase of whose museum and gallery of art already indicates the rapidly approaching necessity of a more ample provision for their accommodation;

" *Therefore,* mindful of their relations and duties to the citizens of New York, who have so liberally sustained all their efforts to place upon an enduring foundation the establishment of this Society as a public institution, whose collections in all departments may be accessible to all classes of the community, subject only to such regulations as may be essential for security and preservation, and anticipating cordial and universal approbation;

" *Resolved,* That a committee of five members, of which the president of the Society shall be a member and requested to act as chairman, be appointed to take such preliminary measures as may be advisable, with a view to securing the State Arsenal and adjoining ground in the Central Park for the museum of the Society."

A special committee was appointed, who secured the approval of the plan by the Commissioners of Central Park, and in 1862 the Society memorialized the Legislature to set apart the Arsenal Building in the Park for the proposed museum.

An act to improve Central Park was passed by the Legislature, March 25, 1862, authorizing the Commissioners to set apart and appropriate to the Society the building known as the New York State Arsenal, with such grounds adjoining as the Commissioners may determine necessary for the purpose of establishing and maintaining by the Society a museum of antiquities and science and a gallery of art. Efforts to secure the necessary funds for the promotion of the plan failed.

In consequence of the low ground and the proximity of the reservoir near the Arsenal Building, the Society urged a change to higher ground in the Park. The Legislature passed an act, April 29, 1868, setting apart for the use of the Society a site in the Park, covering Eighty-first to Eighty-fourth Streets, 300 feet west of Fifth Avenue, the building to be erected at the expense of the Society.

Renewed efforts were made in 1870 to carry out the plan of the Society to establish a museum of history, antiquities, and art, by the erection of a building on the new site in the Park; but owing to the great cost of the proposed building, and the erection of the same on city property, the scheme was finally abandoned.

The Metropolitan Museum of Art occupies this site, the buildings being erected by the city at a cost of $1,000,000, and an annual appropriation from the city of $150,000 for its support.

Mr. Bradish was succeeded in the office of president by Frederic de Peyster, LL.D., who was secretary, 1827-37, and second vice-president, 1850-63, becoming the eleventh president of the Society, January 5, 1864, and serving until 1867. Mr. De Peyster was again elected president (the fifteenth) in 1873, and served until his death, which took place on August 17, 1882, in the eighty-sixth year of his age, at the residence of his son, Gen. J. Watts de Peyster, Tivoli, N. Y.

Frederic de Peyster was born in this city, November 18, 1796. He was a direct descendent of Johannes de Peyster, and son of Frederic de Peyster. He was graduated at Columbia College, 1816. During the War of 1812, he served as a volunteer, with other students of the college, in the erection of fortifications at " McGown's Pass " for the defense of this city. In 1819 he was admitted to the bar, and in 1820 was appointed a Master in Chancery. Shortly after his admission to the bar he was appointed a captain in the One Hundred and Fifteenth Regiment. In 1825 he was aide to Brigadier-General Fleming, and later became a member of Governor De Witt Clinton's staff. He served most faithfully in the boards of management of many charitable and educational institutions, and the instances of his liberal benefactions are numerous on their records.

During a membership in the Society covering fifty-eight years, Mr. de Peyster was its constant and ardent friend, and one of its liberal benefactors. Besides valuable donations of his own, he gave his aid effectually on more than one occasion when the very existence of the Society was at stake. In 1827, Mr. de Peyster, as agent of the Society, successfully appealed to the Legislature for an appropriation for the relief of the institution. The following letter from Mr. de Peyster reports the progress of the bill before the Legislature:

ALBANY, *February* 8, 1827.

SIR: I have the pleasure of informing you that the Senate this day unanimously passed the bill appropriating five thousand dollars for the relief of the New York Historical Society.

The bill was then sent to the House; has been twice read; and is already committed. To effect a favorable result in the Assembly will, I am aware, require a great sacrifice of time and unremitted personal exertion. But animated by my success hitherto, and the fair claims of the Society for legislative aid, I am willing to encounter every obstacle, in the hope and belief of accomplishing the present undertaking.

I have the honor to be, sir, your obt. sevt.,

FREDERIC DE PEYSTER, JR.

DR. DAVID HOSACK,

Pres't N. Y. H. S.

The following resolution was adopted at a meeting held March 13, 1827:

"*Resolved,* That the thanks of this Society be presented to Frederic de Peyster, Jr., Esq., for his zealous, efficient, and disinterested services in proceeding to Albany and presenting to the Legislature the claims of this Society."

The Society celebrated the two hundredth anniversary of the conquest of New Netherland by an address, delivered in the hall of Cooper Union, October 12, 1864, by John Romeyn Brodhead.

The Hon. Hamilton Fish, LL.D., was elected the twelfth president of the Society at an annual meeting held January 2, 1867; and resigned March 29, 1869, to become Secretary of State of the United States.

Mr. Fish was born in this city, August 3, 1808; son of Col. Nicholas Fish. He graduated at Columbia College, 1827; admitted to the bar in 1830; member of Congress, 1843-45; Lieutenant-Governor of New York, 1847-49; Governor, 1849-51; United States Senator, 1851-57; Secretary of State, 1869-77.

After his return to this city Mr. Fish served as first vice-president of the Society from 1881 to 1888, declining a reëlection in consequence of advancing years. He died at Garrisons, New York, September 7, 1893, aged eighty-five years.

The Society is indebted to the munificence of Mr. Thomas J. Bryan for the gift, April 2, 1867, of his noble collection, so well known as the Bryan Gallery of Christian Art, which was arranged and described under his own direction. During a subsequent visit to Europe Mr. Bryan continued his purchases, still further to enrich this gallery, and the zeal and enthusiasm to which the Society is deeply indebted were uninterrupted to the time of his death, May 14, 1870.

Originally this collection was arranged for exhibition on the walls of a spacious room on Broadway, where Mr. Bryan took up his abode in the adjoining chambers. There he could be found, seated in an old-fashioned arm-chair, with his snow-white hair and florid complexion, like some old Venetian or Florentine in his ancestral palace, surrounded with pictorial heirlooms.

He found it impossible to insure his treasures, exposed as they were, without great expense. Often he lamented that there was no public gallery where they would be accessible to the people and perfectly safe. He finally placed his pictures temporarily in the Cooper Union. Six paintings including a miniature of himself by Staigg were stolen from the collection before it was received by the Society; the miniature was subsequently recovered at a curiosity shop.

The splendid results of Mr. Bryan's judicious taste and persevering liberality, thus dedicated to the public in the interest of art, are alike honorable to him, to the Society, and to the city.

The library of the Society was enriched, May 7, 1867, by the addition of the library relating to American history, of the Rev. Dr. Francis L. Hawks, purchased from the family of the Doctor and presented to the Society by Mr. William Niblo. The library is named the "Hawks-Niblo Collection."

At a stated meeting held June 1, 1869, the Rev. Thomas De Witt, D.D., second vice-president, 1840-49, first vice-president, 1850-69, and very active in the advancement of its welfare, succeeded Mr. Fish as the thirteenth president of the Society.

Dr. De Witt was born in Kingston, N. Y., September 13, 1791; died in this city, May 18, 1874. He was graduated at Union College, 1808, and from the Theological Seminary at New

Brunswick, N. J., 1812. The same year he was ordained pastor of the combined congregations of New Hackensack and Hopewell, Dutchess County, N. Y., where he remained until 1827, when he accepted a call to the Collegiate Dutch Church of New York city, of which he was the senior clergyman from 1858 until his death. He was an active director of the Bible, Colonization, Tract, and Sunday-school Societies, as well as the boards of his Church. He was one of the last of the ministers of the Reformed Dutch Church who could preach in the Dutch language.

The Hon. Augustus Schell, first vice-president, and a member of the executive committee since 1845, was elected the fourteenth president of the Society, January 2, 1872.

Mr. Schell was born at Rhinebeck, N. Y., August 1, 1812, the son of Christian and Elizabeth (Hughes) Schell. He graduated with marked distinction from Union College in 1830. He was admitted to the bar of this city, October, 1832. In 1857 he was appointed by President Buchanan Collector of the Port of New York. In 1867 he was elected a member of the Constitutional Convention of the State of New York, and bore a prominent part in its most important labors. In 1872 he was appointed by Governor Hoffman a member of the Commission to propose amendments to the Constitution of the State.

During his half century of active life in New York Mr. Schell was conspicuous in most of the literary, social, and charitable institutions which have been so marked a feature of the period. He was for thirty years a most efficient member of the Board of Trustees of the New York Institution for the Blind, and since 1866 its president.

For nearly half a century Mr. Schell had been one of the most active members of the Society. As one of the executive committee from 1845 to 1872, and its chairman for twenty years, during the period of its most arduous labors and activity, and subsequently during his terms of office as president, Mr. Schell was devoted to the interests of the Society. On January 3, 1883, he was elected the sixteenth president of the Society, and served until his death, March 27, 1884.

The centennial of the Battle of Harlem Heights was celebrated September 16, 1876. The proceedings were under the charge of a Committee of One Hundred of the members of the Society. The guests were received at the Fifth Avenue Hotel, where a collation was provided, and were then escorted by the officers of the Society to the site of the battle-ground, where platforms, gayly decorated with the Continental, Union, State, and city flags, were arranged for their reception. The ground, covered with tents, presented the appearance of an encampment, and from its elevated position commanding extensive views of the North and East rivers, was visible from a great distance, presenting a scene of rare and animated beauty.

The officers and their guests arrived upon the field at the appointed hour, three o'clock in the afternoon, and were closely followed by the

Seventh Regiment New York State Militia, who marched past to the position assigned them, where they halted in military formation.

The meeting was called to order by President de Peyster, who introduced the Rev. Dr. Dix, Rector of Trinity Church, who delivered the invocation, followed by the oration, delivered by the Hon. John Jay. The proceedings were closed by a benediction pronounced by the Rev. William Adams, D.D. The address of Mr. Jay was published, with an historical appendix compiled by Mr. William Kelby.

The one hundredth anniversary of the adoption of the Constitution of the State of New York (April 20, 1877), was celebrated by the Society at the Academy of Music, May 8, 1877. The address was delivered by Mr. Charles O'Conor, on "The Constitutions."

At the meeting of November 1, 1881, the subject of an appropriate celebration by the Society of the centennial anniversary of the evacuation of New York by the British, was referred to the executive committee, who, in a communication to the Mayor and Common Council, called their attention to this event, and expressed the desire of the Society to coöperate with them in a suitable celebration. Subsequently the Chamber of Commerce also asked the city authorities to take action in the matter. The event was celebrated by the city, with the coöperation of the Society, the Chamber of Commerce, and other civic and military bodies.

In 1882, one hundred and fifty paintings of the

most meritorious works of art in the collection of Mr. Louis Durr, a member, were presented to the Society by his executors, in accordance with the terms expressed in his last will. The remainder of his collection was sold, and the proceeds merged in a "Durr Gallery Fund." The Durr collection is especially valuable to the Society in increasing the admirable facilities offered to the student in connection with the "Bryan Gallery."

At an annual meeting held January 6, 1885, Mr. Benjamin H. Field was elected the seventeenth president of the Society.

Mr. Field was born at Yorktown, N. Y., May 2, 1814; died in this city, March 16, 1893. He received his early education at home, and finished his studies at the North Salem Academy. Having decided to go into business he entered the office of his uncle, and in 1832 he became his partner. Among the institutions with which Mr. Field was connected as director or trustee were several banks, the New York Institution for the Deaf and Dumb, the New York Dispensary, and the Eye and Ear Infirmary. He was president of the Home for Incurables at Fordham from the time of its organization until his death.

In 1844 Mr. Field became a life member of this Society; treasurer, 1860-77; second vice-president, 1878-84; for many years a member of the executive committee, and was very active in aiding and securing the necessary funds for the erection of the present edifice.

On December 1, 1885, Mr. John S. Kennedy

submitted a letter from a friend of the Society, stating there was deposited with the Central Trust Company the sum of $100,000, for the purchase of a site and the erection of a building suitable for the purposes of the institution, subject to the condition that the further sum of $300,000 be secured therefor within two years from November 30, 1885.

It being found impossible to raise the amount within the time specified by the donor, Mrs. Robert L. Stuart, the Society requested an extension of twelve months, which was granted. The amount of the sum required by its conditions to be subscribed for the proposed object was reduced from $300,000 to $150,000.

The Hon. John Alsop King was elected the eighteenth president of the Society, January 4, 1887, and became chairman of the committee on subscriptions. Active measures were begun, and through the great exertion and generosity of President King the necessary sum was secured.

Hon. John Alsop King, son of Governor John Alsop King, and grandson of Hon. Rufus King, was born at Jamaica, L. I., July 14, 1817; graduated at Harvard University in 1835; studied the profession of law, and was chosen presidential elector in 1872, and member of the New York State Senate, 1874-75.

Mr. King became a member of the Society in 1881, and in 1887 was elected its president and held that office at the time of his death, November 21, 1900. He delivered the eighty-third anniversary address before the Society. The ability, grace, and dignity which were his characteristics in the discharge of the duties of his office are known to all. Endowed by nature with a kindly and generous disposition, his fine qualities were further developed by a classical education, and by intercourse with the leading men of the world.

During his whole association with The New York Historical Society, either as member or officer, he devoted himself to its interests in a singular degree. To his untiring efforts the Society owes the magnificent site selected for its future home, and it was the dream and hope of his last years that a building worthy of this venerable Society be erected thereon.

The following resolution was adopted, December 4, 1900:

"*Resolved,* That in the death of the Hon. John Alsop King The New York Historical Society laments the loss of an accomplished presiding officer, whose courtesy, tact, and sound judgment have stamped its proceedings with dignity; whose personality contributed largely to its prosperity, and whose unselfish devotion to its interests will be held in grateful memory by every member of this Society."

A memorial of Mr. King was read before the Society, February 5, 1901, by Dean Hoffman.

On May 21, 1889, a special committee was appointed to examine and report on a suitable site for a new building. In answer to an inquiry concerning the possible purchase of the Madison

Avenue front of the Lenox Library, the Trustees of that institution advised the committee that the property was not for sale. It being found that no suitable site on the east side could be secured at a cost within the means of the Society, the committee selected the property situated on Eighth Avenue (Central Park West), consisting of ten city lots, with a frontage of 204 feet 4 inches on the avenue and a depth of 125 feet on Seventy-sixth and Seventy-seventh Streets, respectively. The purchase was effected June 1, 1891.

In consequence of the depression of business throughout the country, the special committee whose appointment was authorized by the Society to solicit subscriptions for the erection of the new building were unable to report any progress until 1899, when subscriptions amounting to $17,000 were received.

On the afternoon of Saturday, April 8, 1893, through the courtesy of the officers and members of the New York Cotton Exchange, the Society assembled in the large hall of the Exchange building, to celebrate the two hundredth anniversary of the introduction of the printing-press in the colony and city of New York, by William Bradford, April 10, 1693. The building of the Cotton Exchange is erected upon the site where the first newspaper was issued. The commemorative address was delivered by Mr. Charlton T. Lewis. To commemorate the event the Society erected two tablets in bronze. The first has been placed at No. 81 Pearl Street, to mark the site where the first printing-office in the city and colony of New York was established, in 1693, and reads as follows:

On This Site
William Bradford
Appointed
Public Printer
April 10, A.D. 1693
Established The First
Printing Press
In The
Colony Of New York
Erected By The
New York
Historical Society
April 10th, A.D. 1893
In Commemoration Of
The 200th Anniversary
Of The Introduction
Of Printing In
New York.

The second tablet was erected on the southeast corner of the New York Cotton Exchange, to mark the site where the first newspaper in New York was printed, in 1725, and read as follows:

On This Site
William Bradford
Appointed Public Printer, April 10th, A.D. 1693
Issued, November 8th, A.D. 1725
The New York Gazette
The First Newspaper Printed In New York
Erected By The
New York Historical Society
April 10th, A.D. 1893
In Commemoration Of the 200th Anniversary Of
The Introduction Of Printing In New York.

These historic sites were located by Mr. William Kelby, late Librarian of the Society, an authority on colonial New York. The Society had previously celebrated, in May, 1868, the two hundredth anniversary of the birthday of William Bradford.

The Very Rev. Eugene Augustus Hoffman, D.D., LL.D., succeeded Mr. King, as the nineteenth president of the Society, January 2, 1901.

Dean Hoffman was born in this city March 21, 1829. He was sixth in descent from Martinus Hoffman, who came from Holland to America in 1657. He graduated from Rutgers College in 1847, and in 1851 from the General Theological Seminary. During the years 1853-79 he was rector of Christ Church, Elizabeth, N. J., St. Mary's, Burlington, N. J., Grace Church, Brooklyn, and St. Mark's, in Philadelphia, respectively. In

1879 he was elected to the office of Dean of the General Theological Seminary, and filled that office until his death. He has left an enduring monument in the growth and prosperity of that institution.

As president of this Society, Dean Hoffman became chairman of the Building Committee, which committee recommended for adoption the plans submitted by Messrs. York and Sawyer, and approved by the Society, October 1, 1901. At this meeting the Society decided to erect the central portion of the new building, 135 by 115 feet. Through the active efforts and personal generosity of Dean Hoffman a large number of subscriptions were secured for the building fund.

The Society, at a meeting held October 7, 1902, adopted the following preamble and resolutions:

"*Whereas,* The New York Society has received the sad intelligence of the death, on June 17, 1902, of the Very Rev. Eugene Augustus Hoffman, D.D, LL.D., D.C.L., president of the Society;

"*Resolved,* That we wish to unite with his kindred and friends in lamenting his decease.

"*Resolved,* That we record with gratitude his great interest in the advancement of the Society's welfare during the years of his membership, ever actively coöperating in furthering the completion of the proposed new building of the Society.

"*Resolved,* That we offer our tribute of high esteem to his memory for his generous gifts to the Society during his lifetime, and are deeply sensible of his lasting interest in our institution as expressed in his latest bequest.

"*Resolved,* That the Society do now adjourn out of respect to the memory of our late president."

An address commemorative of Dean Hoffman was read before the Society, December 2, 1902, by the Rev. Dr. William R. Huntington.

On September 10, 1902, the informal breaking of ground for the new building took place. Mr. Samuel Verplanck Hoffman, son of the late president, raised the first spade of earth, in the presence of the recording secretary, the librarian, and one of the architects. On September 24, 1902, a contract was made for the excavations and foundations for the new building.

Mr. Samuel Verplanck Hoffman was elected the twentieth president of the Society, at an annual meeting held January 6, 1903, succeeding his father, the late Dean Hoffman.

Mr. Hoffman entered upon his duties as president with a determination to carry out the plans of his predecessors to secure for the Society the erection of a suitable building for the proper exhibition of the large collections of the institution.

The foundations for the central portion of the new building were completed, and on November 17, 1903, the officers, members, and guests assembled at two o'clock for the purpose of witnessing the laying of the corner-stone of the Society's new building.

Through the courtesy of the officers of the American Museum of Natural History, the So-

PRESIDENTS

ciety was permitted to assemble in the "Wood Room" of that building, and thence proceeded to the site of the new edifice.

Upon request of the president, the Rev. Charles Edward Brugler delivered the invocation.

The president, in a short address, reviewed the history of the Society from its foundation, and read a list of the articles and publications in the copper box to be placed in the corner-stone.

The corner-stone was then laid by the Hon. Seth Low, LL.D., Mayor of the city of New York.

After the ceremonies the assembly adjourned to the lecture hall of the American Museum of Natural History, to celebrate the ninety-ninth anniversary of the founding of the Society.

The address was delivered by Mr. Hamilton W. Mabie, the subject being "The Genius of the Cosmopolitan City." The exercises concluded with the benediction, pronounced by the Rev. Alexander Hamilton.

On June 2, 1903, the Society amended Section III of the By-Laws, to constitute a new order of membership to be known as Patrons and Fellows. In accordance with this amendment, a diploma for the patrons and fellows of the Society was engraved by Mr. E. D. French, and is 7½ by 9½ inches in size. At the top, in the centre, is an heraldic eagle representing the national character of the Society, while underneath are shields containing the city and State coat of arms, surrounded by a scroll bearing the Society's name. Three medallions give views of the new building, the

Half Moon in the Hudson River being the vignette used on the diploma of the Society, and an early view of New Amsterdam from the original by Block, owned by the Society, together with a suitable inscription.

The one hundredth anniversary of the founding of the Society was celebrated on Tuesday evening, November 22, 1904, by a banquet at Delmonico's.

The banquet hall and dais were decorated with flowers and American flags, and the walls were adorned with the following portraits:

John Pintard, founder.

Hon. Egbert Benson, first president, 1805-15.

Hon. Gouverneur Morris, second president, 1816.

Hon. De Witt Clinton, third president, 1817-19.

Hon. James Kent, fifth president, 1828-31.

Hon. Albert Gallatin, ninth president, 1843-49.

Hon. Luther Bradish, tenth president, 1850-63.

Hon. Frederic de Peyster, eleventh and fifteenth president, 1864-66, 1873-82.

Rev. Thomas De Witt, D.D., thirteenth president, 1869-71.

Hon. Augustus Schell, fourteenth and sixteenth president, 1872, 1883-84.

Benjamin H. Field, seventeenth president, 1885-86.

Hon. John Alsop King, eighteenth president, 1887-1900.

The Very Rev. Eugene Augustus Hoffman, D.D., LL.D., nineteenth president, 1901-03.

Mr. Henry Dexter, Benefactor.

Invitations were extended to the President of the United States, the Secretary of State, the Governor of the State of New York, and Mayor of the city, representatives of historical societies and universities, and delegates of the various patriotic and other societies of this city.

President Roosevelt, Secretary of State John Hay, Bishop Potter, Governor Odell, and Mayor McClellan were unable to be present.

The invocation was pronounced by the Rev. Edward B. Coe, D.D.

The following toasts were offered:

The President of the United States.

The State of New York.

The City of New York.

Our Sister Societies. Charles Francis Adams, LL.D., president of the Massachusetts Historical Society.

America of the Future. Rt. Rev. Henry C. Potter, D.D.

Popular Education. James H. Canfield, LL.D., librarian of Columbia University.

The Twentieth of November. Robert H. Kelby, librarian of the Society.

Hon. Charles V. Fornes, president of the Board of Aldermen, in the absence of the Mayor, responded to the toast, " The City of New York."

A medal in bronze and silver, designed by Mr. Victor D. Brenner, has been struck to commemorate the one hundredth anniversary, showing on the obverse the first president, Egbert Benson, and the founder, John Pintard; on the reverse, the first home of the Society, City Hall, Wall Street, and the new building now in course of erection.

As a fitting sequel to the efforts of the zealous friends of the Society during the past century, it is a pleasure to acknowledge the generous gift, by Mr. Henry Dexter (a member since 1863), of a sum sufficient to insure the erection of the central portion of the new building.

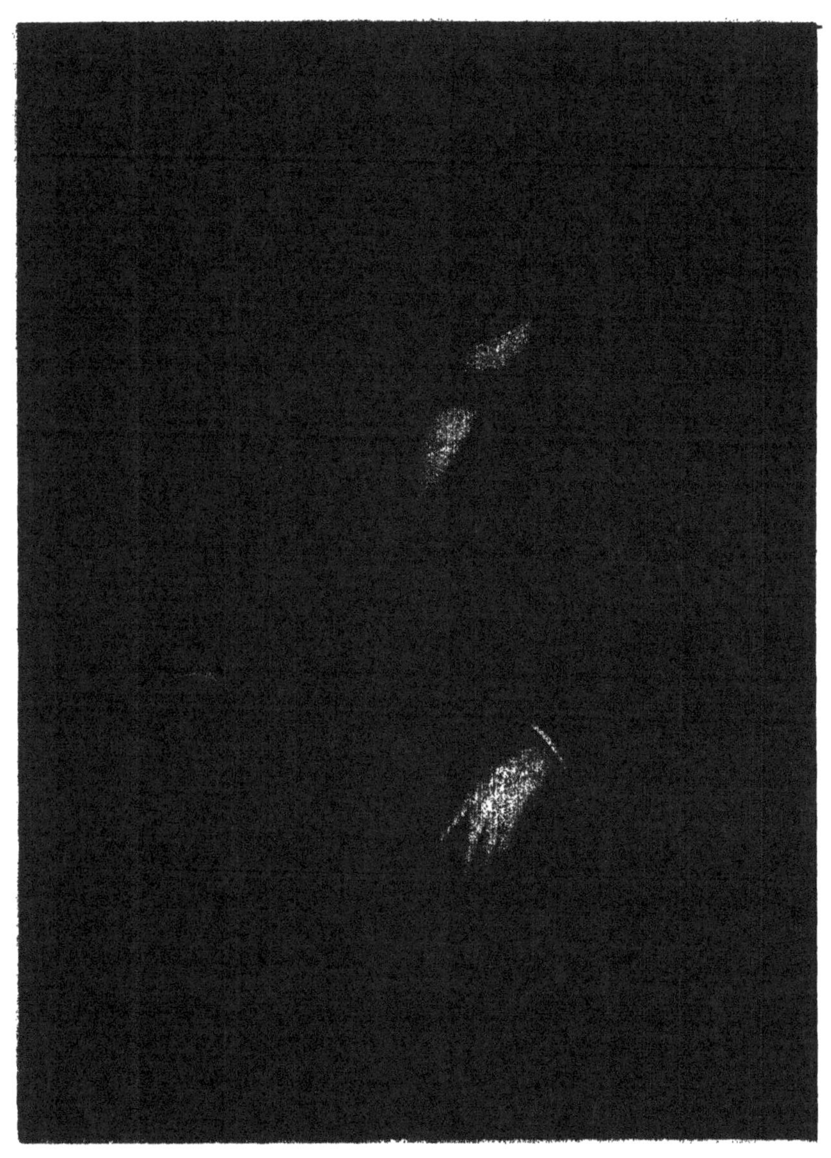

HENRY DEXTER

APPENDIX.

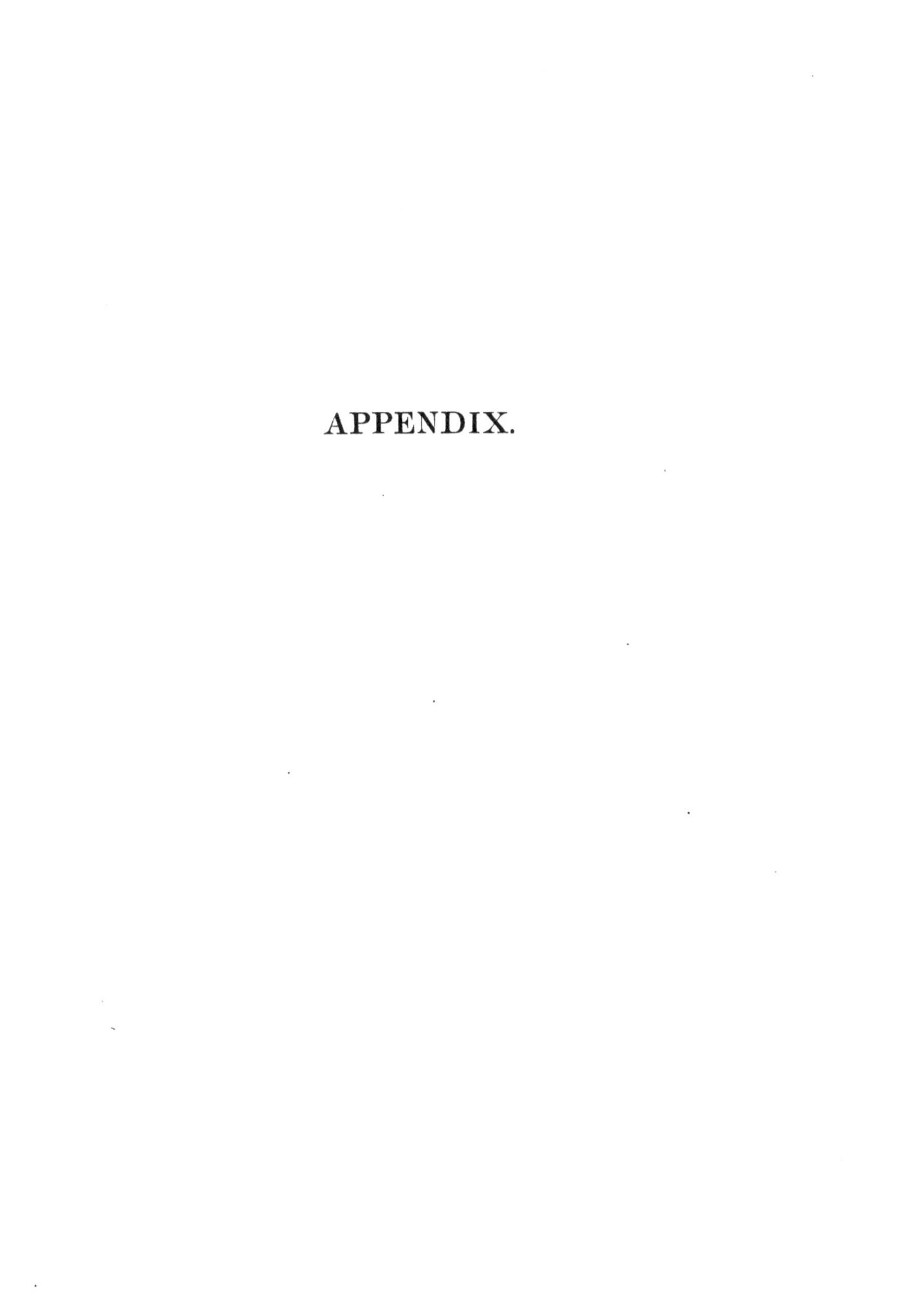

OFFICERS OF THE SOCIETY, 1905.

PRESIDENT,

SAMUEL VERPLANCK HOFFMAN.

FIRST VICE-PRESIDENT,

FREDERIC WENDELL JACKSON.

SECOND VICE-PRESIDENT,

FRANCIS ROBERT SCHELL.

FOREIGN CORRESPONDING SECRETARY,

ARCHER MILTON HUNTINGTON.

DOMESTIC CORRESPONDING SECRETARY,

GEORGE RICHARD SCHIEFFELIN.

RECORDING SECRETARY,

ACOSTA NICHOLS.

TREASURER,

CHARLES AUGUSTUS SHERMAN.

LIBRARIAN,

ROBERT HENDRE KELBY.

EXECUTIVE COMMITTEE.

FIRST CLASS—FOR ONE YEAR, ENDING 1906.

F. ROBERT SCHELL, DANIEL PARISH, Jr.,
FREDERIC WENDELL JACKSON.

SECOND CLASS—FOR TWO YEARS, ENDING 1907.

ISAAC J. GREENWOOD, CLARENCE STORM,
JAMES WILLIAM BEEKMAN.

THIRD CLASS—FOR THREE YEARS, ENDING 1908.

GHERARDI DAVIS, WALTER L. SUYDAM,
FRANK TILFORD.

FOURTH CLASS—FOR FOUR YEARS, ENDING 1909.

JOHN A. WEEKES, J. PIERPONT MORGAN,
GEORGE R. SCHIEFFELIN.

DANIEL PARISH, Jr., *Chairman.*

ROBERT H. KELBY, *Secretary.*

[The President, Vice-Presidents, Recording Secretary, Treasurer, and Librarian are members of the Executive Committee.]

OFFICERS—1805–1905.

OFFICERS OF THE NEW YORK HISTORICAL SOCIETY.

INSTITUTED NOVEMBER 20, 1804. ORGANIZED JANUARY 14, 1805.

PRESIDENTS.

EGBERT BENSON, LL.D....................................1805–1815
GOUVERNEUR MORRIS....................................1816
DEWITT CLINTON, LL.D....................................1817–1819
DAVID HOSACK, M.D., LL.D....................................1820–1827
JAMES KENT, LL.D....................................1828–1831
MORGAN LEWIS....................................1832–1835
PETER GERARD STUYVESANT....................................1836–1839
PETER AUGUSTUS JAY, LL.D....................................1840–1842
ALBERT GALLATIN, LL.D....................................1843–1849
LUTHER BRADISH, LL.D....................................1850–1863
FREDERIC DE PEYSTER, LL.D....................................1864–1866
HAMILTON FISH, LL.D....................................1867–1869
THOMAS DEWITT, D.D....................................1869–1871
AUGUSTUS SCHELL....................................1872
FREDERIC DE PEYSTER, LL.D....................................1873–1882
AUGUSTUS SCHELL....................................1883–1884
BENJAMIN HAZARD FIELD....................................1885–1886
JOHN ALSOP KING....................................1887–1900
EUGENE AUGUSTUS HOFFMAN, D.D., LL.D....................................1901–1902
SAMUEL VERPLANCK HOFFMAN....................................1903–

FIRST VICE-PRESIDENTS.

BENJAMIN MOORE, D.D....................................1805–1809
GOUVERNEUR MORRIS....................................1810–1815
DEWITT CLINTON, LL.D....................................1816
WILLIAM JOHNSON....................................1817
DAVID HOSACK, M.D....................................1818
SAMUEL L. MITCHILL, M.D....................................1819

John Trumbull...1820
Cadwallader D. Colden...1821
Peter Augustus Jay...1824–1827
Philip Hone...1828–1839
William Beach Lawrence...1840–1844
Luther Bradish...1845–1849
Thomas DeWitt, D.D...1850–1869
Gulian C. Verplanck...1870
Augustus Schell...1871
Erastus C. Benedict...1872
William Cullen Bryant...1873–1878
Charles O'Conor...1879–1880
Hamilton Fish...1881–1888
John A. Weekes...1889–1895
J. Pierpont Morgan...1896–1902
Frederic Wendell Jackson...1903–

SECOND VICE-PRESIDENTS.

Brockholst Livingston...1805–1809
DeWitt Clinton, LL.D...1810–1815
William Johnson...1816
David Hosack, M.D...1817
John Trumbull...1818–1819
Anthony Bleecker...1820
John Trumbull...1821–1822
Peter Augustus Jay...1823
John Trumbull...1824–1827
Charles King...1828–1831
Samuel Ward, Jr...1832–1835
William Beach Lawrence...1836–1839
Thomas DeWitt, D.D...1840–1849
Frederic de Peyster...1850–1863
Benjamin R. Winthrop...1864–1867
Gulian C. Verplanck...1868–1869
John A. Dix...1870
Erastus C. Benedict...1871
James William Beekman...1872–1877
Benjamin H. Field...1878–1884
Cornelius Vanderbilt...1885
John A. Weekes...1886–1888
John S. Kennedy...1889–1901
Nicholas Fish...1902
Francis Robert Schell...1903–

FOREIGN CORRESPONDING SECRETARIES.

(Office established March 7 1843.)

Frederic de Peyster....................................1843–1844
John Russell Bartlett....................................1845–1849
Edward Robinson, D.D....................................1850–1862
George Bancroft, LL.D....................................1863–1867
John Romeyn Brodhead, LL.D....................................1868–1870
William Cullen Bryant, LL.D....................................1871–1872
William J. Hoppin....................................1873–1875
George H. Moore, LL.D....................................1876–1878
Erastus C. Benedict....................................1879–1880
John William Draper, M.D., LL.D....................................1881
William M. Evarts, LL.D....................................1882–1887
John Bigelow....................................1888–1895
Eugene Augustus Hoffman, D.D....................................1896–1900
Nicholas Fish....................................1901
Francis Robert Schell....................................1902
Archer Milton Huntington....................................1903–

CORRESPONDING SECRETARIES.

Samuel Miller, D.D....................................1805–1813
David Hosack, M.D....................................1814–1816
John W. Francis, M.D....................................1817–1818
Lyman Spalding, M.D....................................1819–1820
Frederick C. Schaeffer, D.D....................................1821
Henry M. Francis, M.D....................................1822–1826
Frederic de Peyster, Jr....................................1827–1829

(This office was merged in that of Recording Secretary in 1829, and revived in 1838.)

Frederic de Peyster....................................1838–1843

(Name of office changed March 7, 1843, to Domestic Corresponding Secretary.)

George Folsom....................................1843–1844
John Jay....................................1845–1847
James William Beekman....................................1848–1854
Samuel Osgood, D.D....................................1855–1864
John Romeyn Brodhead, LL.D....................................1865–1867
William J. Hoppin....................................1868–1872
Evert A. Duyckinck....................................1873–1878
Edward F. de Lancey....................................1879–1899
Nicholas Fish....................................1900
Frederic Wendell Jackson....................................1901–1902
George R. Schieffelin....................................1903–

RECORDING SECRETARIES.

John Pintard....................1805–1819
John B. Beck, M.D....................1820–1822
Matthew C. Patterson....................1823–1824
Benjamin Haight....................1824–1827
Joseph Blunt....................1828
Frederic de Peyster, Jr....................1829–1837
Benjamin R. Winthrop....................1838
John C. Jay, M.D....................1839
Benjamin R. Winthrop....................1840–1841
Charles Ray King, M.D....................1842
John Jay....................1843–1844
John Bigelow....................1845
Andrew Warner....................1846–1849
Maunsell B. Field....................1850–1853
Andrew Warner....................1854–1899
Sydney H. Carney, Jr., M.D....................1900–1904
Acosta Nichols....................1905–

TREASURERS.

Charles Wilkes....................1805–1818
John Pintard, LL.D....................1819–1827
John Delafield....................1828–1836
Hickson W. Field....................1837–1839
Russell H. Nevins....................1840
Archibald Russell....................1841–1842
Cyrus Mason, D.D....................1843–1847
William Chauncey....................1848–1859
Benjamin H. Field....................1860–1877
Benjamin B. Sherman....................1878–1884
Robert Schell....................1885–1900
Charles A. Sherman....................1901–

LIBRARIANS.

John Forbes....................1805–1809
John Pintard....................1810–1811
John W. Francis, M.D....................1812–1818
Frederick C. Schaeffer, D.D....................1819–1820
Henry M. Francis, M.D....................1821
Matthew C. Patterson....................1822
Henry W. Ducachet, M.D....................1823
Robert Greenhow, M.D....................1824–1826

Richard Ray..1827
James A. Hillhouse...1828
John Delafield, Jr...1829–1830
Samuel Ward, 3d..1831–1835
Joseph Blunt...1836–1839
George W. Folsom...1840–1841
George Gibbs...1842–1847
Jacob B. Moore...1848
George H. Moore..1849–1875
John Austin Stevens..1876–1878
Jacob B. Moore...1879–1887
Charles Isham..1888–1892
William Kelby..1893–1898
Robert H. Kelby..1898–

STANDING COMMITTEE.

William Johnson..1805–1815
Samuel L. Mitchill, M.D....................................1805–1818
David Hosack, M.D..1805–1813
John M. Mason, D.D...1805–1817
Daniel D. Tompkins...1805–1808
John McKesson..1805–1817
Anthony Bleecker...1805–1819
DeWitt Clinton...1808–1809
Gulian C. Verplanck..1810–1827
Peter Augustus Jay...1814–1820
Samuel F. Jarvis, D.D......................................1816
James Eastburn...1817–1819
John G. Bogert...1818–1820
Jacob Morton...1818
John McKesson..1819–1820
Joseph W. Brackett...1819–1820
John W. Francis, M.D.......................................1820–1828
Thomas Eddy..1820–1821
Anthony Bleecker...1821–1827
William Gracie...1821–1828
Matthew C. Patterson.......................................1821
Henry W. Ducachet, M.D.....................................1821–1822
Zachariah Lewis..1822–1823
Ezra Weeks...1822
William L. Stone...1823–1824
John H. Beck, M.D..1823–1824
William Cooper...1824

Joseph Blunt....................................1825–1827
Robert C. Sands....................................1825
James E. DeKay, M.D....................................1825
Henry Brevoort....................................1828
William Sampson....................................1828
Hugh Maxwell....................................1828
Matthew C. Patterson....................................1828
Samuel Ward....................................1828

(This Committee was abolished by an amendment of the Constitution of the Society, January 9, 1829.)

COMMITTEE ON PRINTED PUBLICATIONS.

Francis L. Hanks, D.D....................................1837–1838
Frederic de Peyster....................................1837–1839
Henry M. Francis, M.D....................................1837–1838
George Folsom....................................1839
John L. Stephens....................................1839–1841
George Gibbs....................................1841
Archibald Russell....................................1841
John Russell Bartlett....................................1841
John Neilson, Jr., M.D....................................1842

COMMITTEE ON MANUSCRIPTS.

George B. Rapelye....................................1837
Gouverneur Morris Wilkins....................................1837–1839
George Folsom....................................1837–1838
Archibald Russell....................................1839
George Gibbs....................................1839
John Knox, D.D....................................1840–1841
William W. Campbell....................................1840–1842
Prosper M. Wetmore....................................1841–1842
Henry R. Schoolcraft....................................1842

(The above Committees were succeeded by an Executive Committee, November 1, 1842.)

EXECUTIVE COMMITTEE.

Cyrus Mason, D.D.	1842–1847
Prosper M. Wetmore	1842–1848
George Folsom	1842
John Jay	1842–1847
Frederic de Peyster	1842–1866
Gulian C. Verplanck	1843–1845
Edward Robinson, D.D.	1843–1862
John L. Stephens	1843
Alexander W. Bradford	1843–1845
William L. Stone	1843
Erastus C. Benedict	1843–1848
Albert Gallatin	1843–1849
William Beach Lawrence	1843–1845
Thomas DeWitt, D.D.	1843–1871
George Gibbs	1843–1848
Henry R. Schoolcraft	1845–1847
John Romeyn Brodhead	1845–1872
Augustus Schell	1845–1884
Luther Bradish	1845–1863
John Bigelow	1845
John Russell Bartlett	1845–1849
James William Beekman	1846–1854
Andrew Warner	1846–1899
William Chauncey	1848–1869
Jacob B. Moore	1848
William W. Campbell	1849
Marshall S. Bidwell	1849–1857
George H. Moore	1849–1892
Benjamin H. Field	1849–1893
Francis L. Hawks, D.D.	1849–1889
Charles H. Russell	1850
Maunsell B. Field	1850–1855
Erastus C. Benedict	1851–1880
Benjamin R. Wintrhop	1855–1867
Samuel Osgood, D.D.	1855–1879
George Folsom	1858–1868

Benjamin W. Bonney....................................1860–1867
George Bancroft..1863–1867
Charles P. Kirkland...................................1864–1883
George Gibbs..1864–1867
Robert L. Stuart..1864–1866
William Tilden Blodgett.............................1867–1874
John Adriance...1867–1873
Hamilton Fish..1867–1869
Evert A. Duyckinck....................................1868–1878
James William Beekman..............................1868–1877
Robert Lenox Kennedy................................1869–1887
Edward F. de Lancey..................................1869–1900
William R. Martin......................................1870–1873
John Taylor Johnston..................................1872–1886
Frederic de Peyster....................................1873–1882
Joseph B. Varnum......................................1873–1874
Henry Drisler...1874–1876
James H. Titus...1874–1879
John Austin Stevens....................................1875–1878
Jacob D. Vermilye......................................1877–1885
William Dowd..1877–1888
Benjamin B. Sherman..................................1878–1884
Jacob B. Moore..1879–1887
Joseph W. Patterson...................................1880–1881
John A. Weekes..1880–1900
Royal Phelps...1881–1884
William Libbey...1881–1887
John C. Barron, M.D..................................1881–1886
Willard Parker, Jr., M.D...........................1881–1887
Robert Schell...1885–1900
John W. C. Leveridge.................................1885–1896
John S. Kennedy...1885–1900
Daniel Parish, Jr...1886–
Charles H. Russell, Jr.................................1887–1898
John Alsop King...1887–1900
Charles Isham..1888–1902
Frederic Gallatin..1888–1898
George W. Vanderbilt.................................1889–1902
J. Pierpont Morgan.....................................1889–
Francis Tomes..1890–1897
William Kelby..1892–1898
Isaac J. Greenwood.....................................1895–
John J. Tucker..1897–1902
Robert H. Kelby...1898–
Frederic Wendell Jackson............................1899–

Nicholas Fish..1900–1902
Francis Robert Schell.................................1900–
A. V. W. Van Vechten..................................1900
Sydney H. Carney, Jr., M.D............................1900–1904
Eugene Augustus Hoffman, D.D..........................1901–1902
Charles Frederic Hoffman, Jr..........................1901–1902
Charles A. Sherman....................................1901–
John A. Weekes, Jr....................................1902–
George R. Schieffelin.................................1902–
Frank Tilford...1902–
Samuel Verplanck Hoffman..............................1903–
Clarence Storm..1903–
James William Beekman.................................1903–
Gherardi Davis..1904–
Walter L. Suydam......................................1904–

MEMBERS.

HONORARY MEMBERS.

Name	Place	Year
Alden, Timothy	Massachusetts	1810
Allen, William	"	1810
Adams, John	"	1813
Adams, John Quincy	"	1813
Austin, David	Connecticut	1813
Austin, Capt. Henry		1817
Anderson, Andrew	Scotland	1818
Allston, Washington	Massachusetts	1819
Aspinwall, Thomas	England	1819
Adams, Jasper	South Carolina	1836
Arfwedson, Charles David	Sweden	1840
Alexander, James Eward	England	1842
Antinori, C. Vincenzio	Italy	1842
Amici, Vincenzo	"	1842
Amici, C. Giovanni B.	"	1842
Arista, Mariano	Mexico	1842
Anderson, Robert	U. S. A.	1861
Anderson, Alexander, M.D	New York	1868
Adams, Charles Francis	Massachusetts	1871
Arthur, Chester Alan	New York	1881
Bard, Samuel	New York	1810
Brown, Charles Brockden	Pennsylvania	1810
Buckminster, Joseph S.	Massachusetts	1810
Bozman, John Leeds	Maryland	1811
Buchan, Earl of	Scotland	1813
Banks, Sir Joseph	England	1813
Bostock, John	"	1813
Bloomfield, Joseph	New Jersey	1813
Boudinot, Elias	"	1813
Boudinot, Elisha	"	1813
Bentley, William	Massachusetts	1813
Beck, Theodoric Romeyn	New York	1813
Bradford, Alden	Massachusetts	1813
Bradbury, John	England	1816
Brown, Jacob	Washington, D. C.	1817
Brewster, David	Scotland	1817

Name	Place	Year
Busby, Charles A.	England	1817
Brackenridge, Henry W.		1817
Blatchford, Samuel		1818
Botta, Carlo	Italy	1818
Brown, Francis	New Hampshire	1819
Binney, Horace	Pennsylvania	1819
Bowditch, Nathaniel	Massachusetts	1821
Beck, Lewis C.		1821
Birdseye, Victory	New York	1827
Barstow, Gamaliel H.	“	1827
Buckline, David W.	“	1827
Bancroft, George	“	1839
Bethune, George W.	Pennsylvania	1839
Blythe, Calvin	“	1839
Barlow, Timothy	Illinois	1840
Bacon, Leonard	Connecticut	1840
Brignole di Brunnhoff, John	Italy	1842
Burci, Charles	“	1842
Berrien, John McPherson	Georgia	1844
Baldwin, Roger S.	Connecticut	1846
Burnet, Jacob	Ohio	1849
Barrundia, José	Central America	1852
Buchanan, James	Pennsylvania	1855
Bowring, Sir John	England	1858
Bryant, William Cullen	New York	1860
Bryan, Thomas J.	“	1865
Burlingame, Anson	Massachusetts	1868
Bigelow, John	New York	1869
Bismarck-Schönhausen, Otto Edward Leopold	Germany	1890
Clinton, George	New York	1810
Correa de Serra, José	Portugal	1813
Clark, Adam	England	1813
Chisholm, Colin	“	1813
Cooper, Thomas	Pennsylvania	1813
Coffin, Charles	Tennessee	1813
Cogswell, Joseph	Massachusetts	1813
Carmichael, Dr.	Mississippi	1816
Cogswell, Joseph G.	Massachusetts	1816
Cochran, William	Nova Scotia	1817
Chauncey, Isaac		1818
Chase, Philander	Ohio	1818
Corsini, Prince		1819
Carter, Nathaniel H.	New Hampshire	1819
Chauncey, Charles	Connecticut	1819

Croswell, Edwin	New York	1827
Carroll, Charles H.	"	1827
Carroll, Charles, of Carrollton	Maryland	1828
Curry, William Wallace		1832
Cushing, Caleb	Massachusetts	1837
Channing, William E.	"	1839
Cogswell, William	"	1840
Condit, John S.	New Jersey	1841
Carrillo, Cura Don E.	Yucatan	1843
Cass, Lewis	Michigan	1844
Cogswell, Jonathan	Connecticut	1844
Clarkson, Thomas	England	1844
Cochrane, Andrew W.	Canada	1846
Choate, Rufus	Massachusetts	1852
Clark, Myron H.	New York	1855
Capponi, Marquis Gino	Italy	1858
Cornell, Alonzo B.	New York	1880
Cleveland, Grover	"	1883
Davis, John	Massachusetts	1810
Dwight, Timothy	Connecticut	1810
Duer, William A.	New York	1813
Duncan, Andrew, jr.	England	1813
De Lisle, Alire R.	France	1813
Dunbar, Elijah	New Hampshire	1813
Davidson, Richard	Mississippi	1816
Dickerson, Mahlon	New Jersey	1816
Dewar, Henry	Scotland	1817
Duponceau, Peter S.	Pennsylvania	1819
Dinsmore, Silas	New Hampshire	1819
Durand, Asher B.	New York	1821
Dalhousie, Earl of	Scotland	1823
Drake, Samuel G.	Massachusetts	1838
Dunn, Henry	England	1839
Davies, C. S.	Maine	1841
Dod, Albert B.	New Jersey	1841
Davidson, Robert	"	1843
Day, Thomas	Connecticut	1843
Dix, John A.	New York	1848
Draper, John William	"	1865
Dewey, George	U. S. N.	1898
Davidson, Randall Thomas	England	1904
Eliot, John	Massachusetts	1810
Ebeling, Christoph Daniel	Germany	1816
Eddy, Samuel	Rhode Island	1819

Name	Place	Year
Edelcrantz, Baron	Sweden	1821
Evans, David E.	New York	1827
Everett, Edward	Massachusetts	1839
Elton, Romeo	Rhode Island	1839
Ericsson, John	New York	1862

Name	Place	Year
Freeman, James	Massachusetts	1810
French, Jonathan	New Hampshire	1813
Franklin, William T.	England	1816
Fromentin, Eligius	Louisiana	1818
Ferdinand III.	Tuscany	1819
Fossombrini, Vittoria		1819
Farmer, John	New Hampshire	1819
Featherstonehaugh, G. W.	England	1821
Fine, John	New York	1827
Foote, Elial Todd	"	1827
Flagg, Azariah C.	"	1827
Fenner, James	Rhode Island	1828
Felt, Joseph B.	Massachusetts	1839
Friederichstahl, Le Chev.	Austria	1840
Force, Peter	Washington, D. C.	1845
Fillmore, Millard	New York	1850
Field, Cyrus W.	"	1858
Fish, Hamilton	"	1859
Fenton, Reuben E.	"	1865

Name	Place	Year
Gibbs, George	Rhode Island	1810
Gahn, Henry	Denmark	1813
Good, John Mason	England	1813
Gore, Christopher	Massachusetts	1813
Gorham, John	Massachusetts	1813
Green, Ashbel	New Jersey	1816
Garden, Alexander	South Carolina	1817
Galusha, Jonas	Vermont	1818
Gregoire, Abbé	France	1818
Gallizioli, Filippo		1819
German, John F.	Pennsylvania	1826
Greig, John	New York	1827
Gardiner, David	"	1827
Granger, Francis	"	1827
Gaines, Edmund P.	Virginia	1827
Gordon, Thomas F.	New Jersey	1833
Greene, George W.	Rhode Island	1839
Gräberg de Hemsö J.	Sweden	1841
Gray, Francis C.	Massachusetts	1843
Gilpin, Henry D.	Pennsylvania	1844

Gayarre, Charles	Louisiana	1845
Grant, Ulysses S.	U. S. A.	1865
Grote, George	England	1866
Gladstone, William E.	"	1879
Garfield, James A.	Ohio	1881
Hazard, Ebenezer	Pennsylvania	1810
Holmes, Abiel	Massachusetts	1813
Hoffman, George F.	Germany	1813
Haygarth, John	England	1813
Humphreys, David	Massachusetts	1813
Harris, Thaddeus M.	"	1813
Hall, John E.	Pennsylvania	1817
Hitchcock, Edward	Massachusetts	1817
Hawkins, Samuel		1818
Hurlburt, M. L.	South Carolina	1818
Harby, Isaac	"	1818
Hartmann, C. F. A.	Germany	1819
Humboldt, Alexander	Prussia	1820
Henry, William	England	1820
Hay, William, jr.	New York	1827
Hunt, Montgomery	"	1827
Hawley, Gideon	"	1827
Hoyt, Epaphras	Massachusetts	1842
Hamilton, Sir William	Ireland	1843
Herschel, Sir John	England	1843
Hodgson, William B.	Georgia	1843
Horne, Thomas H.	England	1847
Hornblower, Joseph C.	New Jersey	1849
Hunt, Washington	New York	1850
Hoffman, John T.	"	1869
Hayes, Rutherford B.	Ohio	1879
Harrison, Benjamin B.	Indiana	1889
Higgins, Frank Wayland	New York	1905
Ireland, William M.		1817
Ives, Eli	Connecticut	1819
Ingraham, Joseph H.	Mississippi	1840
Johnson, William S.	Connecticut	1810
Jefferson, Thomas	Virginia	1813
Jenner, Edward	England	1813
Jones, Samuel		1813
Jackson, James	Massachusetts	1813
Jeffrey, Francis	Scotland	1813
Jameson, Robert	"	1817

Johnson, William	South Carolina	1818
Jamieson, Robert		1819
Jordan, Ambrose L.	New York	1827
Johnson, Alexander B.	“	1827
Jackson, Andrew	Tennessee	1833
Julius, N. C.	Germany	1836
Jonge, Jongheer J. C. de	Netherlands	1842
Jomard, M.	France	1842
James, George P. R.	England	1850
Johnson, Andrew	Tennessee	1865
Kirkland, John T.	Massachusetts	1810
Kent, James	New York	1813
Kendall, James	Massachusetts	1814
Kemper, Jan Melchior	Netherlands	1817
Knight, Thomas A.		1823
Kirkland, Joseph	New York	1837
King, Jonas	Greece	1865
Lettsom, John C.	England	1813
L'Escalier, Baron	France	1813
Lowell, Charles	Massachusetts	1813
Low, James		1813
Lambrechtsen, N. S.	Netherlands	1816
Lee, William	Washington	1817
Lewis, Morgan	New York	1821
Lafayette, Marquis de	France	1824
Lafayette, George W.	“	1824
Lansing, Derrick	New York	1827
Lemon, Robert	England	1843
Lelewel, Joachim	France	1845
Lincoln, Abraham	Illinois	1861
Laboulaye, Edward	France	1864
Longfellow, Henry Wadsworth	Massachusetts	1897
Murray, Lindley	England	1810
Morse, Jedidiah	Massachusetts	1810
McKean, Joseph	“	1810
Mease, James	Pennsylvania	1810
Madison, James	Virginia	1813
Muhlenbergh, Henry	Pennsylvania	1813
Mellen, John	Massachusetts	1813
Michaux, André	France	1816
Maclure, William		1817
Murray, John	Scotland	1817
Monroe, James	Virginia	1817

Marbois, Barbé	France	1818
Mossell, S. Amos	Pennsylvania	1818
Magini, Dr		1819
Milnor, James	New York	1819
Moulton, Joseph W	"	1824
Marcy, William L	"	1827
Moseley, Daniel	"	1827
Magnusen, Finn	Denmark	1838
Moore, Richard C	Virginia	1839
Milledoler, Philip	New Jersey	1839
Murdock, James	Connecticut	1839
McIlvaine, C. P	Ohio	1840
Markoe, Francis, jr	Washington	1841
Morpeth, Viscount	England	1843
Murray, Charles Augustus	England	1844
Marsh, George P	Vermont	1848
MacGregor, John	England	1855
Motley, John Lothrop	Massachusetts	1856
Morse, Samuel F. B	New York	1858
Morgan, Edwin D	"	1859
Milman, Henry Hart	London	1860
McClellan, George B	U. S. A	1862
McKinley, William	Ohio	1897
Nason, Reuben	Maine	1813
Nichols, Ichabod	"	1813
Neil, Patrick	Scotland	1817
Norman, B. M	Louisiana	1843
Navarette, M. F. de	Spain	1844
Ogden, Aaron	New Jersey	1816
Oakley, Thomas J	New York	1819
Ombrosi, James	Italy	1819
O'Callaghan, Edmund B	New York	1876
O'Conor, Charles	"	1881
Odell, Benjamin B., jr	"	1901
Pearson, George	England	1813
Putnam, Rufus	Ohio	1813
Prince, John	Massachusetts	1813
Peck, W. Dandridge	"	1813
Pierce, John	"	1813
Pickering, Timothy	"	1814
Prescott, Samuel J	"	1814
Peale, Charles Wilson	Pennsylvania	1817
Plumer, William	New Hampshire	1817

Perkins, Cyrus	New Hampshire	1819
Puccini, Aurelio		1819
Persoon, C. W	France	1819
Pazos, Vicente		1819
Porter, Peter B	New York	1827
Pitcher, Nathaniel	"	1827
Pickering, John	Massachusetts	1839
Prescott, William H	"	1839
Pennington, William	New Jersey	1841
Pitkin, Timothy	Connecticut	1843
Perez, Juan Pio	Yucatan	1843
Polk, James K	Tennessee	1845
Poussin, William Tell	France	1848
Paez, José A	Venezuela	1850
Pierce, Franklin	New Hampshire	1853
Pedro II	Emperor of Brazil	1856
Peabody, George	England	1857
Quincy, Josiah	Massachusetts	1810
Rush, Benjamin	Pennsylvania	1810
Ramsay, David	South Carolina	1810
Roxburgh, William	India	1813
Roscoe, William	England	1813
Rush, Richard	Pennsylvania	1813
Rumford, Count	France	1813
Randolph, Edward	Mississippi	1816
Roberdeau, Isaac	Pennsylvania	1817
Riley, James		1817
Ridolfi, Marquis Cosimo		1819
Robertson, William D		1820
Rudd, John C	New York	1827
Root, Erastus	"	1827
Rafn, C. C	Denmark	1838
Reed, William B	Pennsylvania	1839
Robbins, Thomas	Connecticut	1843
Ritter, Carl	Germany	1844
Raumer, Frederick Von	"	1844
Ranké, Leopold	"	1844
Ramirez, José Fernando	Mexico	1863
Rosencrans, William S	U. S. A	1865
Rives, William C	Virginia	1867
Robinson, Lucius	New York	1877
Roosevelt, Theodore	"	1899
Reid, Whitelaw	"	1905

Smith, S. Stanhope	New Jersey	1810
Sinclair, Sir John	Scotland	1813
Smith, James E.	England	1813
Smith, Isaac		1813
Shaw, William S.	Massachusetts	1813
Story, Joseph	"	1813
Steinhauer, H.	Pennsylvania	1816
Stewart, Walter		1816
Southey, Robert	England	1816
Smith, William	Canada	1816
Stockton, Richard	New Jersey	1816
Smith, Charles H.	Netherlands	1817
Schaeffer, F. D.	Pennsylvania	1817
Swainson, James	England	1817
Steel, John H.		1817
Storer, Clement	New Hampshire	1818
Stansbury, Arthur		1818
Stewart, Charles		1818
Stickney, J. B.		1818
Serriestori, M.		1819
Schoolcraft, Henry Rowe		1819
Sabine, Edward	England	1822
Stewart, Arch-deacon	Canada	1824
Sparks, Jared	Massachusetts	1826
Spencer, John C.	New York	1827
Sill, Theodore	"	1827
Starkweather, Samuel	"	1827
Sutherland, Jacob	"	1827
Stevens, Samuel	"	1827
Savage, John	"	1827
Stebbins, Charles	"	1827
Smith, Gerrit	"	1827
Schwartz, John G.		1837
Staples, William R.	Rhode Island	1838
Savage, James	Massachusetts	1839
Sullivan, William	"	1839
Stevens, William Bacon	Georgia	1840
Simms, W. Gilmore	South Carolina	1843
Salva, Jayme	Spain	1844
Spencer, Ambrose	New York	1847
Swain, David L.	North Carolina	1847
Scott, Winfield	Virginia	1850
Seymour, Horatio	New York	1853
Seward, William H.	"	1858
Smith, Goldwin	England	1864

Sherman, William T.	U. S. A.	1865
Stanley, Arthur Penrhyn	England	1869
Simon, Jules	France	1890
Trumbull, Benjamin	Connecticut	1810
Teignmouth, Lord	England	1813
Thouin, André	France	1813
Thomas, Isaiah	Massachusetts	1813
Treadwell, John D.	"	1813
Trevett, Samuel R.		1813
Tappan, Benjamin	Maine	1813
Thomson, William A.		1817
Tappen, Christopher, jr.		1818
Trullani, Leonardi		1819
Tallmadge, James	New York	1827
Tallcott, Samuel A.	"	1827
Tracy, Albert H.	"	1827
Taylor, John W.	"	1827
Tyler, John	Virginia	1841
Ternaux-Compans, H.	France	1842
Tefft, J. K.	Georgia	1843
Thonching	China	1843
Taylor, Zachary	Louisiana	1849
Tilden, Samuel J.	New York	1875
Toreno, Conde de	Spain	1878
Uberto dei Nobili, Chev.		1819
Vallancey, Charles	Ireland	1813
Vaughan, Benjamin	Maine	1813
Van Royen, Henricus	Netherlands	1817
Vander Palme, Joh. Hen.	"	1817
Vander Kemp, Fr. A.		1818
Vaughan, John	Pennsylvania	1819
Van Schaack, Peter	New York	1827
Viele, John	"	1827
Vroom, Peter D.	New Jersey	1840
Vanden Brook, J. W.	Amsterdam	1842
Van Rensselaer, Stephen	New York	1846
Van Buren, Martin	"	1847
Vanden Brink, R. C. Bakhuizen	Netherlands	1857
Webster, Noah	Connecticut	1810
Wistar, Caspar	Pennsylvania	1810
Warren, John C.	Massachusetts	1813
Williams, Samuel	Vermont	1813

Winthrop, James..........................Massachusetts.........1813
Winthrop, William.........................   " 1813
Wheelock, John...........................New Hampshire.......1813
Wilson, Joshua L.........................Ohio.................1813
Willson, James...........................Pennsylvania..........1813
Woods, Leonard...........................Massachusetts.........1813
Wallace, Joshua M........................New Jersey...........1813
Wilkinson, James..1816
Warden, David B..........................France...............1816
Williams, Stephen W......................Massachusetts.........1818
Williams, Charles........................Vermont..............1819
Walsh, Robert............................Pennsylvania..........1820
Wilson, John.............................Scotland..............1821
Watson, John F...........................Pennsylvania..........1823
Wood, Silas..............................New York............1824
Wright, Silas............................   " 1827
Williams, Nathan.........................   " 1827
Waterman, Thomas G.......................   " 1827
Woodworth, John..........................   " 1827
Wilkeson, Samuel.........................   " 1827
Wadsworth, James.........................   " 1827
Watts, Charles...........................Louisiana.............1828
Winthrop, Adam...........................   " 1836
Winthrop, Thomas L.......................Massachusetts.........1837
Webb, Thomas H...........................Rhode Island.........1838
Williamson, William D....................Maine................1839
Willis, William..........................   " 1839
Wilkes, Charles..........................New York............1842
Williams, Sir John B.....................England..............1843
Wall, Garrett D..........................New Jersey...........1844
Westbrook, Cornelius D...................New York............1844
Webster, Daniel..........................Massachusetts.........1847
Woolsey, Theodore Dwight.................Connecticut...........1858
Winthrop, Robert C.......................Massachusetts.........1859
Walworth, Reuben H.......................New York............1866
Waite, Morrison R........................Ohio.................1877

Young, Samuel............................New York............1827
Young, Alexander.........................Massachusetts.........1841

PATRONS.

✠Bruce, Catherine Wolfe.
Bruce, Matilda Wolfe.
✠Clark, Alfred Corning.
Dexter, Henry.
✠Hoffman, Eugene Augustus, D.D.
Hoffman, Samuel Verplanck.
Huntington, Archer Milton.
✠Jones, John Divine.
Kennedy, John S.
✠King, John Alsop.
Morgan, J. Pierpont.
✠Mount, Charlotte A.
Mount, Susan.
✠Schell, Mrs. Augustus.
Schell, F. Robert.
✠Schell, Robert.
✠Schermerhorn, William C.
Sherman, Charles A.
✠Stuart, Mrs. Robert L.
Thompson, Mrs. Frederick F.
✠Vanderbilt, Cornelius.
Vanderbilt, George W.

✠Deceased.

PATRONS

By Succession.

Baker, Charlotte S.
Clark, Stephen Carlton.
Hoffman, Mrs. Eugene Augustus.
Maccaffil, Charlotte Mount.
Schermerhorn, Frederic Augustus.
Vanderbilt, Alfred Gwynne.

FELLOWS.

Astor, William Waldorf.
Auchmuty, Mrs. Richard T.
✠Austin, William.
✠Avery, Samuel P.
✠Babcock, Samuel D.
Baker, George F.
✠Banyer, Goldsborough.
Beekman, Gerard.
Billings, Frederick.
Bliss, Cornelius N.
✠Bliss, George.
Clark, Edward S.
✠Constable, James M.
✠Cook, Henry H.
Cutting, R. Fulton.
Cutting, W. Bayard.
✠Delano, Franklin H.
✠Dows, David.
✠Dubois, Abram, M.D.
Ely, Ambrose K.
Fahnestock, Harris C.
✠Fayerweather, Daniel B.
✠Field, Benjamin H.
✠Fish, Nicholas.
Greene, Martin E.
Greenwood, Isaac J.
✠Herrman, Henry.
Herrman, Mrs. Henry.
✠Hoffman, Mrs. Charles Frederick.
Hoffman, Mrs. Eugene Augustus.
✠Hoyt, Charles A.
✠Huntington, Collis P.
✠Iselin, Adrian.
Isham, William B.
Jackson, Frederic Wendell.
Jackson, Theodore F.
Jackson, William H.
Jesup, Mrs. Morris K.
✠Kennedy, Rachel L.
King, Mary Rhinelander.
Langdon, Woodbury G.
Lanier, Charles.
Lawton, Mrs. James M.
✠Livingston, Robert J.
✠Marquand, Henry G.
Mills, Darius O.
Morton, Levi P.
Parish, Daniel, jr.
Parsons, Mrs. John E.
Phipps, Henry.
Phœnix, Lloyd.
Phœnix, Phillips.
✠Potter, Orlando B.
✠Pyne, Percy R.
✠Rhinelander, Julia.
Rhinelander, Serena.
✠Rogers, Mrs. Charles H.
✠Skidmore, William L.
Sloan, Samuel.
Sloane, William D.
Speyer, James.
✠Stewart, David.
Stokes, Caroline Phelps.
Storm, Clarence.
Sturges, Frederick.
Thorne, Phebe Anna.
✠Tiffany, Charles L.
Tilford, Frank.
Vanderbilt, William K.
Von Post, Herman C.
✠Weekes, John A.
White, Mrs. Joseph M.
✠Williams, George G.
✠Winthrop, Robert.

✠Deceased.

ANNUAL AND LIFE MEMBERS—1905.

Abbe, Cleveland 1880
†Abbe, Mrs. Robert 1897
†Abeel, George 1896
†Adams, Edward D 1904
†Adee, George Augustus 1857
†Adee, Philip H 1857
†Aldrich, Mrs. James Herman . . 1902
†Alexander, Charles Beatty 1896
Alexander, John Franklin 1871
Anderson, John, jr 1902
†Andrews, Blanche L 1887
†Andrews, James B 1857
†Andrews, William L 1857
Anjou, Gustave 1903
†Appleby, Charles E 1857
°†Astor, William Waldorf 1879
°†Auchmuty, Mrs. Richard T . . 1901
Augustine, Clark Bell 1904
†Avery, Samuel P., jr 1903
Aymar, Benjamin 1898
Ayres, Stephen Beckwith 1902

†Bacon, Charlotte V 1888
Bacon, Leon Brooks 1902
Baker, Charles, jr 1903
Baker, Frederic 1898
°Baker, George F 1879
Balch, Collins L 1901
Baldwin, George V. N 1888
†Ball, Thomas R 1902
Banks, David, jr 1898
Banks, James Lenox 1896
Banta, Theodore M 1887
Barclay, David 1901
†Barger, Milton S 1896
†Barger, Samuel F 1883
†Barnes, Cora F 1903
Barney, Charles T 1902
†Barron, John C., M.D 1864
Bartlett, Franklin 1880
†Barton, Oliver Grant 1857
Baylies, Edmund L 1893
°†Beekman, Gerard 1875
†Beekman, James William 1886
Beekman, John Neilson, M.D . . 1897
Beekman, Mrs. William B 1902
†Belcher, Henry W 1857
†Bell, Jared Weed 1897
†Belmont, August 1902
†Belmont, Oliver H. P 1888
†Belmont, Perry 1857
†Benedict, Erastus C 1867
†Benedict, Henry H 1902
†Benedict, James 1864
†Benkard, Henry R 1857
†Benson, Charles B 1905
†Benson, Egbert 1888
†Benson, Robert 1887
Berwind, Edward J 1901
Betts, Frederick H 1875
†Betts, George W 1857
†Bevan, Llewelyn D., D.D . . . 1880
†Bickmore, Albert S 1869
†Bigelow, Poultney 1889
†Bigelow, L. Horatio 1903
°†Billings, Frederick 1893
Bingham, George F 1903
†Bishop, Cortlandt Field 1871
†Bishop, David Wolfe, jr 1875
Bishop, Louis Faugères, M.D . . 1905
Bispham, William 1903
†Bissell, Rev. Pelham St. G 1887

°†Bliss, Cornelius N. 1877
†Bliss, Cornelius N., jr. 1897
†Bogert, Henry Lawrence. 1892
Bolton, Reginald Pelham. 1902
Bond, Frank S. 1893
Bookstaver, Henry W. 1869
†Boorman, J. Marcus. 1854
Bostwick, Henry A. 1897
Bosworth, Mrs. Francke H. 1902
Boucher, Charles. 1900
†Bowen, Clarence W. 1885
†Breese, Eloise Lawrence. 1902
Brett, Cornelius, D.D. 1905
Brewster, Charles O. 1902
Brewster, Samuel Dwight. 1900
†Briggs, Charles A., D.D. 1884
Britton, Charles P. 1893
†Brodhead, Eugenia. 1874
†Brooks, Emerson. 1899
Brower, John L. 1905
Brower, William L. 1880
Brown, Rev. Abbott. 1892
Brown, Addison. 1863
Brown, Charles Hilton. 1904
†Brown, Edward F. 1875
†Brown, Egerton. 1875
Brown, J. Romaine. 1905
Brown, John Crosby. 1873
†Brown, John Potts. 1852
†Brown, Robert I. 1851
†Browning, J. Hull. 1903
Brownne, John S. 1901
*†Bruce, Matilda Wolfe. 1871
†Brugler, Rev. Charles Edward. 1904
†Budd, Mrs. William A. 1902
Buchman, Albert. 1905
Bulkley, Edward Addison. 1902
Bulkley, Edwin M. 1905
Bull, Charles C. 1897
†Bull, Robert Maclay. 1902
†Bull, William Lanman. 1900
†Burdge, Franklin. 1880
Burgess, Edward S. 1903
†Burrell, David J., D.D. 1896
†Burton, Thomas J. 1901
Butler, Emily O. 1902
Butler, Nicholas Murray. 1905

†Cameron, Mrs. A. Scott. 1896
†Cannon, Henry W. 1895
†Carhart, Amory Sibley. 1882
Carney, Sydney H., jr., M.D. . . . 1893
†Carpender, William. 1892
†Carpenter, Charles L. 1904
†Carroll, Royal Phelps. 1888
†Carter, Henry C. 1901
Carter, James C. 1867
†Castree, John W. 1902
†Chamberlain, Daniel Drew. . . . 1857
Chamberlain, Jacob Chester. . . . 1899
Chamberlain, Leander T., D.D. 1897
Chapman, Henry T. 1901
†Chauncey, Elihu. 1882
†Chauncey, Henry. 1857
†Cheesman, T. Matlack, M.D. . 1904
Chew, Beverly. 1898
Clark, Alzamore H. 1905
°†Clark, Edward S. 1901
†Clark, Henry Austin. 1899
†Clark, William A. 1895
Clarke, Charles L. 1897
Clarke, George C. 1896
†Clarkson, Banyer. 1892
†Clarkson, Margaret Livingston 1885
†Clarkson, Matthew. 1853
Clinch, Edward S. 1897
†Clute, Rev. Robert F. 1857
Cochrane, John W. 1874
†Codman, Ogden, jr. 1904
Cohn, Adolphe. 1903
†Cole, Edward F. 1904
†Coles, Henry Rutgers Remsen. 1894
Coles, Jonathan Ackerman, M.D. 1901
Collamore, Marion Davis. 1896
Collier, Peter F. 1905
†Collier, Price. 1905
†Collyer, Robert, D.D. 1882
Comfort, Randall. 1905
†Comstock, Frederick H. 1889
Conkling, Nathaniel W., D.D. . . 1883

†Constant, Samuel Victor......1893
†Cook, Arthur Peters..........1864
Cook, Charles T..............1877
°†Cook, Henry H.............1882
Cooper, Edward.............1850
Cooper, Theodore.............1895
†Corlies, Joseph W., jr.........1851
Cotton, Louis Kossuth.........1903
†Coxe, Macgrane.............1898
†Crane, Albert................1873
Crane, Frank W...............1897
Crane, Warren C..............1896
†Crimmins, John D...........1899
Cromwell, David W...........1904
†Crosby, Ernest Howard.......1884
†Cross, Mrs. C. Vanderbilt.....1903
†Cruikshank, Warren..........1905
Cummings, George F..........1882
†Curtis, William Edmund......1901
Cushman, Norman............1905
°Cutting, R. Fulton............1888
°†Cutting, W. Bayard..........1888

Darlington, Charles Francis....1902
†Dart, Russel................1855
†Davenport, Mrs. Ira..........1905
Davies, Julien T..............1880
Davies, William Gilbert........1877
Davis, Chandler...............1903
†Davis, Fellowes..............1896
Davis, Gherardi..............1894
†Davis, Mrs. Gherardi.........1889
†Davis, John W. A............1903
†Davis, Vernon M............1903
Dayton, Charles W............1897
Debevoise, George............1903
De Bost, William L...........1905
†De Forest, Robert Weeks......1866
†De Kay, Charles.............1881
†Delafield, Albert.............1891
†Delafield, Joseph Livingston...1893
†Delafield, Julia Livingston....1891
†Delafield, Maturin Livingston.1874
†Delafield, Maturin Livingston, jr.........................1899
Delafield, Richard............1901
†De Lancey, Edward Floyd....1851
Delano, Warren, jr............1896
Delmonico, L. Crist...........1902
†De Luze, Philip Schuyler......1895
†De Meli, Henry G. D.........1895
Depew, Chauncey M..........1869
†De Peyster, C. Augusta.......1902
†De Peyster, Elizabeth V. R....1902
†De Peyster, Frederic J........1852
†De Peyster, John Watts.......1850
†De Peyster, Wm. Moore Dongan1897
De Puy, Henry F.............1902
†Derby, Richard H., M.D......1882
†De Witt, William G..........1889
*†Dexter, Henry..............1862
Dexter, Stanley W.............1897
†Dey, Anthony................1863
†Dey, J. Warren Scott.........1865
†Dey, Richard Varick.........1895
†Deyo, Robert E..............1897
†Dibble, William A............1857
Dill, Josephine H.............1903
Dimond, Thomas.............1901
Dininny, Ferral C.............1902
Dix, John Adams............1905
Dix, Morgan, D.D............1879
†Dixon, George, jr............1857
†Dodd, John M., jr............1894
Dodd, Samuel C. T............1894
†Dodge, Anson G. P...........1870
Dodge, Cleveland H...........1883
†Dominick, Marinus Willett....1896
†Dornin, William C...........1862
Douglas, William H...........1901
†Dows, Tracy.................1905
Dresser, D. Le Roy...........1902
Drummond, I. Weyman.......1905
Dugro, P. Henry..............1891
†Duncan, William B...........1857
Dunning, William A...........1900
†Du Pont, Henry A...........1905
Duryee, Joseph Rankin, D.D...1902
Dwight, Frederick............1904
†Dwight, Rev. Melatiah Everett1900

Eaton, Bradley L. 1901
†Eaton, Sherburne Blake. 1877
†Edmonds, John Worth. 1894
†Einstein, Lewis. 1902
†Eliot, Ellsworth, M.D. 1865
†Elliott, Frederick B. 1857
Elseffer, Mrs. William L. 1897
°†Ely, Ambrose K. 1857
Embury, Aymar. 1872
Emmet, Thomas Addis, M.D. . . 1864
†Eno, Amos F. 1888
†Evans, William T. 1896
†Everson, George. 1857

°Fahnestock, Harris C. 1879
†Fairchild, Charles S. 1882
†Faye, Thomas. 1871
†Field, Cortlandt de Peyster. . . . 1850
†Field, Mrs. Cortlandt de Peyster. 1885
†Fish, Mrs. Nicholas. 1901
†Fish, Stuyvesant. 1875
Fitzgerald, James. 1905
Fleitmann, Ewald 1903
†Folsom, George W. 1858
Forbes, Rev. Elmer Severance. . 1896
Ford, Worthington C. 1892
†Foster, Frederic de Peyster. . . . 1874
Foster, Scott. 1902
†Foulke, Bayard Fish. 1903
†Fox, Austen G. 1872
†Francis, Valentine Mott, M.D. 1858
Fraser, Horatio N. 1899
Freedman, John J. 1873
French, Amos Tuck. 1888
†Frenche, James. 1853
Friend, Meyer M. 1902
Frissell, Algeron S. 1903
Frye, Jed 1902
Fuller, Frank. 1892

†Gallatin, Albert. 1905
†Gallatin, Albert Eugene. 1903
†Gallatin, Frederic. 1870
†Gallatin, R. Horace. 1892
Galot, Alphonse. 1877
Gardiner, Asa Bird. 1871
Gawtry, Lewis B. 1904
†Gebhard, William H. 1868
†Geer, Walter. 1902
Geissenhainer, Jacob A. 1881
†Gibbs, Theodore Kane. 1891
Gibson, George Rutledge. 1902
†Gihon, John. 1857
†Gihon, William. 1852
Gilder, Richard Watson. 1881
†Giles, Stephen W. 1896
Gilsey, Frederick C. 1905
Glenney, William P. 1905
†Glover, Mrs. James A. 1886
†Goodwin, James J. 1891
†Gould, Edwin. 1896
†Grant, R. Suydam. 1857
Gray, John Clinton. 1873
†Greene, Alister. 1896
Greene, Edward. 1875
†Greene, John W., M.D. 1854
°Greene, Martin E. 1870
Greene, Richard Henry. 1896
†Greenough, John. 1891
°Greenwood, Isaac J. 1858
Greenwood, Langdon, jr. 1893
†Gregory, Charles. 1902
†Gregory, Henry E. 1886
†Griffen, Benjamin. 1874
†Griffith, Daniel J. 1901
†Guggenheim, Murray. 1901
†Gunther, John Jacob. 1904

Hackstaff, Charles L. 1898
†Hackstaff, Mrs. Charles L. 1903
†Hadden, John Aspinwall. 1866
†Haines, Samuel B. 1877
Haldane, Mary H. 1903
Hall, Edward Hagaman. 1902
Hall, Frank Oliver, D.D. 1905
†Hall, Mary F. 1901
Halpin, Francis. 1891
†Halsey, Frederick R. 1900
Halsey, Richard T. H. 1896

Hamilton, Edmond H. 1890
Hamilton, William Gaston 1889
†Harbeck, Charles John 1897
†Harbeck, Charles T. 1857
Hardley, J. Wheeler 1902
Harison, Mrs. George D. L. 1897
Harper, Francis P. 1897
†Harper, John 1885
†Harriman, Edward Henry 1885
Harris, William H. 1903
Hasbrouck, Mrs. Frederick 1900
Haskell, J. Amory 1895
Hatch, Albert J. 1870
†Havemeyer, Frederic C. 1899
†Havemeyer, Henry O. 1899
†Havemeyer, John C. 1857
†Havemeyer, William F. 1891
†Havens, Henry P. 1882
†Hawes, Gilbert Ray 1895
†Hawkes, McDougall 1898
†Hawley, Thomas R. 1864
Headley, Russel 1901
Healey, Warren M. 1888
†Hearn, George A. 1895
Heminway, Homer 1882
†Hendricks, Albert 1869
†Herrick, John J. 1852
°†Herrman, Mrs. Henry 1889
†Hess, Selmar 1903
Higgins, Eugene 1889
†Higginson, James J. 1899
Hill, Charles B. 1901
Hill, Edward Bruce 1896
Hillhouse, Charles B. 1897
Hine, Charles Gilbert 1905
Hinman, William K. 1863
†Hinton, John H., M.D. 1877
Hitchcock, Ripley 1905
Hobbs, Frederick G. 1902
†Hoe, Robert, jr. 1852
Hoffman, Charles Frederick, jr. . 1903
Hoffman, Mrs. Charles F., jr. . . . 1903
Hoffman, Charles Gouverneur . . 1905
*°†Hoffman, Mrs. Eugene A. . . . 1901
*†Hoffman, Samuel Verplanck . . 1901
†Hoffman, Mrs. Samuel Verplanck 1903
Hoffman, William M. V. 1897
Hoffman, Mrs. William M. V. . . 1903
†Holden, Edwin B. 1900
†Holden, James C. 1855
Holland, Joseph 1899
†Hopkins, George B. 1902
Hoppin, William Warner 1871
Hotchkin, Walter D. 1905
Hubbell, George W. 1895
†Hunter, Frederick W. 1882
*†Huntington, Archer Milton . . . 1890
Huntington, Charles R. 1896
†Huntington, Daniel 1846
Huntington, Frederick J. 1881
Huntington, William R., D.D. . 1884
Hurlbut, Theodore D. 1893
†Hurry, Renwick Clifton 1903
Hutchinson, Cary T. 1894
†Hutchinson, William J. 1877
†Hyatt, Abram M. 1902
†Hyde, Clarence M. 1891
Hyde, Edwin Francis 1891
Hyde, Frederick E., M.D. 1892
Hyde, Henry St. John 1904
†Hyde, James H. 1903
Hyman, Mrs. David M. 1902
†Hyslop, George L., M.D. 1866

Ireland, John B. 1886
Irving, Walter 1890
°†Iselin, Adrian 1863
†Iselin, Adrian, jr. 1868
†Iselin, Columbus O'Donnel . . . 1873
Iselin, William E. 1873
†Isham, Charles 1885
°†Isham, William B. 1885
†Ives, Brayton 1905

Jackson, Charles Fred. Havemeyer 1899
°†Jackson, Frederic Wendell . . . 1892
†Jackson, Rev. Samuel M. 1888
°†Jackson, Theodore F. 1897

°†Jackson, William H. 1898
Jacobi, Abraham, M.D 1872
Jaffray, Robert 1890
†Jarvis, Jay 1863
†Jay, William 1852
†Jennings, Oliver G 1893
Jesup, Morris K 1854
°†Jesup, Mrs. Morris K 1888
†Johnson, Henry W 1852
Johnston, Henry P 1882
†Johnston, J. Herbert 1897
†Johnston, John H 1862
Joline, Adrian H 1893
†Jones, Charles Landon 1900
†Jones, Rev. Henry L 1857
†Jones, James H 1882
Jones, Mrs. Oliver Livingston . . 1902
†Jordan, Stanley 1900
Judge, John H 1902

Kane, S. Nicholson 1897
†Kelby, Charles Hendre 1899
†Kelby, Robert Hendre 1893
†Kelby, Thomas 1891
Kelley, Frank Bergen 1904
*†Kennedy, John S 1883
†Kennin, John L 1863
Kent, William 1896
†Keteltas, Alice 1902
Keys, Alice M 1905
†King, Mrs. Charles Ray 1902
†King, Edward 1888
†King, Ellen 1889
†King, George Gordon 1898
†King, John Alsop 1900
°†King, Mary Rhinelander 1889
Kip, William F 1901
†Kirtland, Anna T. E 1865
Kohler, Max J 1903

Lacombe, E. Henry 1904
†Lane, Smith E 1850
°†Langdon, Woodbury G 1878
°†Lanier, Charles 1857
†Lansing, Mrs. Abraham 1904
Larkin, John 1895
†Lathrop, Edward, D.D 1854
Lawrence, Richard H 1900
†Lawson, Leonidas M 1874
°Lawton, Mrs. James M 1900
Leaycraft, J. Edgar 1887
†Le Boutillier, Charles 1896
Leeds, Henry 1905
Leeds, William 1905
†Lefferts, Marshall C 1903
†Leggett, Francis H 1901
†Leggett, Francis W 1902
†Leland, Charles H 1879
Lesher, Arthur L 1884
Levussove, Moses S 1905
Levy, Elias Henry 1881
Lewis, John N 1897
†Libbey, Jonas Marsh 1877
†Libbey, Mrs. William 1877
†Libbey, William, jr 1880
†Lincoln, James M 1891
Lindsay, John D 1904
Livermore, John R 1904
†Livingston, Johnston 1883
†Livingston, William S., jr 1879
†Lockman, De Witt M 1890
†Lockman, John T 1884
Loewy, Benno 1894
†Logan, Walter S 1892
Loomis, Archibald G 1902
Lord, Franklin B 1902
Lord, Joseph E. P 1900
†Loring, Daniel A 1887
†Loubat, Joseph F 1871
†Low, Joseph T 1901
†Low, Seth 1890
Ludlow, James B 1901
Lufburrow, Elizabeth S 1903
†Lummis, William 1877
†Lund, Dagny Engelsted 1905
†Lynch, James D 1882
Lyon, A. Maynard 1902

†McAlpin, Charles W 1902
McCafferty, Robert 1894

McCagg, Louis Butler.........1900
McCall, John A...............1899
†McClintock, Emory..........1895
†McCord, William H..........1902
McCoun, Henry T............1902
†McKesson, George Clinton....1873
†McKesson, Irving............1899
†McKesson, John, jr..........1857
McKim, Robert V............1898
†McLanahan, George W.......1882
†Maclay, Isaac Walker........1878
McLean, Donald.............1899
McLellan, Charles Woodberry....................1905
McLellan, Hugh..............1905
†Macy, Nelson...............1902
Madison, Winfield S...........1904
Madison, Mrs. Winfield S......1904
Maginnis, William H..........1905
Mahler, Edward J............1876
†Maitland, Alexander.........1886
†Mallet-Prevost, Severo........1901
†Mallett, Edward J...........1856
Man, William................1890
†Markoe, Francis H., M.D.....1889
Marks, George Edwin.........1896
†Marquand, Allan............1886
†Marquand, Henry...........1881
Marsh, John Edward..........1896
†Marshall, Louis..............1905
Martin, Susan Tabor..........1893
Mather, Frank J., jr...........1901
Maury, Charles W............1891
Maury, Henry T..............1891
Meeks, Edwin B..............1889
†Merrall, William J...........1875
†Merritt, Douglass............1867
†Mersereau, John W..........1857
†Mersereau, Nicholas R........1857
Messenger, Maria Gerard......1893
Meyrowitz, Emile B...........1901
†Miller, George Macculloch....1881
†Miller, M. Rumsey...........1901
†Milliken, David..............1857
°Mills, Darius O..............1902
†Mitchell, Albert M. P.........1890
†Mitchell, Benjamin G........1902
Mitchell, Edward.............1903
†Mitchill, Bleecker N..........1884
Moffat, George Barclay.......1905
Moffat, R. Burnham...........1898
†Moldenke, Rev. Charles E....1886
Moller, Peter.................1901
†Montgomery, Thomas H......1874
†Moore, Jacob B..............1878
Moore, William H. H..........1852
Moran, Charles...............1903
†Moreau, Charles C...........1861
Morgan, George H............1881
*Morgan, J. Pierpont..........1881
Morgan, Junius Spencer.......1902
†Morison, John A.............1867
†Morrell, William H...........1865
Morris, Fordham.............1870
†Morris, Henry Lewis.........1874
†Morris, Newbold.............1901
†Morrison, David M..........1857
†Morrison, George Austin......1892
†Morrison, William E.........1857
†Morse, Charles W...........1902
°Morton, Levi P..............1855
Moss, Frank.................1905
†Mossman, John M...........1884
Mott, Hopper Striker..........1902
*†Mount, Susan.............1882
Munsell, Charles E............1892
Murray, J. Archibald..........1885
Myers, Edward...............1896

Nash, John McLean...........1902
Nash, William Alexander.......1902
†Navarro, José F. de..........1880
Neeser, John G...............1905
Neill, Henry Harmon..........1903
†Nelson, William.............1893
†Nesbitt, George F...........1857
†Nichols, Acosta.............1903
Nichols, Anthony Dey.........1903
†Nichols, Effingham H........1892
Nichols, George Livingston....1897

†Nickerson, Mrs. Thomas W., jr.........................1903
†Nisbet, William F............1900
Noble, Francis L..............1903
†Norrie, Ambrose Lanfear.....1888
†Norrie, Adam Gordon........1888
†Norrie, Gordon..............1852
†Norrie, Van Horne, M.D......1888
Norton, Edward L............1894

†Oakley, Henry A.............1848
†Oakman, Walter G...........1896
Odell, Hamilton..............1863
Odell, Hammond.............1899
Oettinger, Sigmund...........1902
Ogden, Henry A..............1893
†Ogden, William B...........1887
†Oglesby, Mrs. Joseph H......1904
Olcott, J. Van Vechten.........1897
Olcott, Mrs. J. Van Vechten....1903
†Opdyck, Leonard E..........1888
†Orvis, Charles Eustis.........1903
†Orvis, Edwin W.............1903
Osgood, Herbert L............1893
†Osgood, John C.............1890
Oudin, Lucien................1900

Paddock, Eugene H...........1891
†Page, Edward D.............1893
Paige, Edward Winslow........1893
°†Parish, Daniel, jr............1882
†Parish, Henry...............1901
†Parish, Wainwright..........1901
†Parker, Mrs. Gilbert..........1888
†Parker, Willard, M.D.........1857
Parris, Edward L.............1880
†Parsons, John E.............1901
°†Parsons, Mrs. John E........1877
†Parsons, William Decatur.....1895
Patton, Charles L.............1892
Peck, Charles E..............1901
†Peck, Guy Dayton...........1895
†Peckham, Walton M.........1857
†Pell, Frederick Aycrigg.......1877
†Pell, Howland...............1889
Pell, John L. E...............1903
†Pelletreau, William S.........1899
†Penfold, Edmund............1852
†Penfold, William Hall........1857
Perkins, J. Deming............1859
Perry, Alexander..............1903
Peters, Mrs. Edward McClure..1902
†Peters, Samuel T.............1886
†Peters, William Richmond....1904
Phillips, N. Taylor............1894
°Phipps, Henry................1901
°†Phœnix, Lloyd..............1887
°†Phœnix, Phillips............1887
Piderit, Marie Alma...........1900
Platt, Frank H................1890
Plympton, Gilbert Motier......1897
Poillon, William..............1905
Poor, Henry W...............1891
†Post, Abram S...............1884
†Post, Henry A. V............1888
Potter, Frederick..............1902
†Potter, Rt. Rev. Henry C., D.D......................1868
Powell, William R.............1902
Powell, Wilson M.............1865
Pratt, Dallas B...............1897
†Prentice, William P..........1867
†Prime, William C............1859
Prince, J. Dyneley............1903
Prince, Mrs. J. Dyneley........1903
Proctor, William Ross.........1902
Pryer, Charles.................1877
Purdon, John................1895
Purdy, J. Harsen..............1903
Putnam, Frederic Ward........1899
†Pyle, James Tolman..........1902
†Pyne, M. Taylor.............1888

Quintard, Edward, M.D.......1895
Quintard, George W...........1861

Rainey, Thomas, M.D.........1900
Randell, James Wells..........1905
†Ransom, J. Henry...........1865
†Raven, Anton A.............1901

†Read, Harmon Pumpelly......1885
†Read, John Meredith, jr......1885
†Read, William A..............1901
†Redmond, Mrs. Henry S......1889
†Reed, Josiah H...............1865
Reid, Wallace.................1904
†Rhinelander, Frederic W., jr..1894
Rhinelander, Philip...........1890
†Rhinelander, Rev. Philip Mercer.........................1888
°†Rhinelander, Serena..........1888
Rhinelander, T. J. Oakley.....1896
†Rhinelander, William.........1857
Rhoades, John Harsen.........1869
Rhoades, Lyman..............1893
†Rich, Joseph S................1903
Richards, Jeremiah............1899
Richardson, Rosell L..........1895
Riker, John Jackson...........1891
†Riker, John L................1850
†Riker, Samuel................1888
†Rives, George L..............1891
†Robb, J. Hampden...........1872
†Robinson, James A...........1852
†Roche, Rev. Spencer S........1887
Rock, Matthew................1902
†Rockefeller, John D., jr.......1901
†Roelker, Alfred..............1882
†Romaine, Louis T............1902
†Roosevelt, Robert B., jr.......1890
Root, Elihu...................1873
Rothschild, Jacob.............1891
†Rowell, George P.............1870
†Rowland, H. Edwards........1874
Rowland, Thomas Fitch.......1863
Rusch, Henry A...............1898
†Russell, Archilbald D.........1874
†Russell, Charles Howland.....1884
Ruthrauff, Charles C..........1904
†Rutter, Robert................1887
Ryer, Frederick Ridabock......1896
†Ryno, Crowell H.............1867

†Sabin, Joseph F..............1892
Sackett, Henry Woodward.....1904
Salter, Wm. Tibbits...........1859
Sanford, George B............1905
†Sanford, Henry G............1903
†Sanxay, Theodore F..........1904
Satterlee, F. Le Roy, M.D......1887
Sawyer, Philip................1901
†Schell, Edward H............1883
*†Schell, F. Robert............1867
†Schell, Mrs. F. Robert........1902
Schermerhorn, Charles A.......1883
†Schieffelin, George R.........1894
Schieffelin, Schuyler...........1890
†Schieffelin, William Jay.......1904
†Schiff, Jacob H...............1889
Schroeder, J. Langdon.........1901
†Schuyler, Philip..............1876
Schwab, Gustav H............1888
Scott, Edward W..............1902
Scudder, Moses L.............1897
Scudder, Willard..............1893
†Seaman, Louis Livingston, M.D......................1903
†Servoss, George Hancock.....1856
†Seton, Alfred L..............1857
†Seton, Robert, D.D...........1883
Seymour, Morris Woodruff.....1895
Shaler, Alexander.............1867
Sheldon, James O.............1885
*†Sherman, Charles A.........1888
†Sherman, Mrs. Charles A.....1902
†Sherman, Corinne A..........1904
†Sherman, George............1884
†Sherman, John T............1889
†Sherman, William Watts......1902
†Sherwood, S. Clinton.........1904
Sherwood, Samuel............1892
†Shirley, Rufus George........1905
Short, Edward Lyman.........1903
†Shrady, John, M.D...........1865
Sickles, Daniel E..............1896
†Siegel, Mrs. Henry...........1902
†Silliman, Charles A...........1863
†Silliman, Harper.............1904
†Sistare, William H. M........1870
Slade, Mrs. William Gerry.....1903

†Slawson, George L. 1902
°†Sloan, Samuel 1902
†Sloane, Charles W 1877
†Sloane, Thomas O'Conor 1877
°†Sloane, William D 1873
†Sloane, William Milligan 1898
Smith, Alfred H 1902
Smith, Chandler 1904
†Smith, Charles H. L 1857
†Smith, Cornelius B., D.D 1867
†Smith, George Williamson, D.D 1900
Smith, Hiram 1895
Smith, Isaac P 1905
†Smith, J. Augustus 1904
Smith, James Henry 1898
Smith, L. Bayard 1901
†Smith, S. Newton 1904
†Smith, Stephen, M.D 1867
†Smith, Thomas E. V 1888
Smith, Walter M 1885
Smith, Wm. Alexander 1858
†Smith, William W 1903
†Smith, William Wheeler 1854
†Smull, Thomas 1857
Smyth, Herbert C 1896
†Southmayd, Charles F . . . . 1864.
Spears, Harry D 1895
Speir, Archibald W 1901
°†Speyer, James 1901
†Spofford, Paul N 1845
Squires, Grant 1905
Stanton, Mrs. John 1896
Stanton, Lucius M 1905
Stearns, John Noble 1882
†Steers, James R 1897
Steinmuller, George A 1905
†Sterling, Charles Burr 1897
†Stevens, Byam K 1863
Stevens, Rev. C. Ellis 1905
Stevens, Edward L 1905
†Stevens, Frederic W 1903
†Stevens, John Austin 1848
†Steward, John, jr 1857
Stewart, John A 1850
Stewart, Wm. Rhinelander 1894
†Stillman, James 1887
Stillwell, John Edwin, M.D 1901
†Stimson, Daniel M., M.D 1903
Stimson, Mrs. Daniel M 1897
†Stokes, Anson Phelps 1891
°†Stokes, Caroline Phelps 1889
†Stokes, I. N. Phelps 1900
†Stokes, James 1864
Stone, Mason A 1902
°†Storm, Clarence 1902
†Storm, Edna Graham 1903
†Storm, Mabel Louisa 1903
†Straus, Oscar S 1884
Sturges, Henry C 1874
°†Sturges, Frederick 1880
†Sturges, Rev. Isaac C 1904
Sturgis, Frank K 1900
Sturgis, Mrs. Frank K 1900
†Stuyvesant, A. Van Horne 1857
†Stuyvesant, Robert Reade 1857
†Stuyvesant, Robert V. R 1857
Stuyvesant, Rutherfurd 1869
†Suckley, Robert B 1896
†Suydam, Walter L 1903
†Swan, Edward H., jr 1881
†Swan, Otis D 1850

Taber, Harriette 1905
†Tailer, Edward Neufville 1898
Taintor, Charles N 1905
Talcott, Rev. J. Frederick 1901
†Tallmadge, William C 1864
†Taylor, George C 1857
†Taylor, Henry R 1905
†Taylor, Theodorus B 1851
Tenney, Charles H 1903
Tenney, Daniel G 1895
†Terhune, Thomas 1861
†Terry, Roderick, D.D 1882
Thompson, David W 1902
†Thompson, Frederick Diodati . 1866
*†Thompson, Mrs. Frederick F. 1901
†Thompson, Walter Ledyard . . . 1896
Thorn, Leonard Mortimer 1874

†Thorne, Jonathan............1857
°†Thorne, Phebe Anna........1891
†Thorne, Samuel.............1902
†Thorne, Wm. Van Schoonhoven.....................1897
†Tiemann, Hermann N........1899
°†Tilford, Frank..............1902
†Tinker, James...............1871
Todd, Charles Burr...........1890
Toler, William P..............1902
†Tolles, Brainard.............1901
Tompkins, Calvin.............1905
Tompkins, Hamilton B........1874
Tooker, Gabriel Mead.........1861
Totten, William H. B..........1897
Towne, Paul R...............1904
Townsend, Mrs. Edward M....1900
Townsend, Howard...........1890
Townsend, S. DeLancey, D.D..1902
†Trask, Spencer...............1905
†Treadwell, George A.........1892
Treat, Edward A..............1900
†Treat, Erastus B.............1893
†Trevor, Henry Graff..........1893
Tuck, Edward................1877
†Tucker, Edwin..............1900
†Tucker, Mrs. John J.........1902
†Tucker, Walter Curtis........1900
Tweedie, M. Stanley..........1904

Ulmann, Albert...............1903

†Van Alstyne, Lawrence.......1895
Van Amringe, Guy............1903
Van Amringe, John Howard....1903
Van Beuren, Henry S..........1892
Van Cortlandt, Augustus.......1884
*†Vanderbilt, George W.......1884
°†Vanderbilt, William K.......1878
Vander Veer, Albert, M.D......1905
Van De Water, George R., D.D.1904
Van Hoesen, George M........1885
†Van Nest, Mrs. Alexander T...1902
Van Norden, Warner..........1902
Van Rensselaer, A. Cortlandt...1898
†Van Rensselaer, Mrs. John King......................1898
Van Rensselaer, Mrs. Schuyler.1902
Van Slyck, George Finch.......1900
†Van Slyck, George W.........1871
†Van Vechten, A. V. W........1858
†Van Woert, Francis G........1857
Vermilye, Ashbel G., D.D......1893
Vermilye, Daniel B............1903
Ver Planck, William G.........1896
Villard, Oswald Garrison......1898
†Vincent, Marvin R., D.D.....1901
°†Von Post, Herman Casper....1895

Waddington, George..........1890
†Wagner, Frederic C..........1903
Wait, William B., jr...........1893
†Walker, Alexander...........1903
†Walker, Rt. Rev. Wm. D., D.D.......................1865
Wandell, Francis Livingston....1904
Wandell, Townsend...........1889
†Ward, Edmund A............1883
Ward, Francis E..............1902
†Ward, Henry Marion.........1901
†Ward, J. Otis...............1861
†Ward, Sylvester L. H.........1893
Warren, William R...........1902
†Waterbury, John I...........1894
†Watson, Rev. J. Henry........1902
†Watson, Mrs. J. Henry.......1903
†Watts, George Burghall.......1863
†Webb, Wm. Seward, M.D....1882
†Webster, David, M.D........1889
†Webster, Sidney.............1867
†Wedemeyer, Arnold J. D......1885
†Weekes, Alice Delano.........1900
†Weekes, Henry de Forest......1895
†Weekes, John A.............1883
†Welch, Alexander M..........1896
†Welles, Edgar T.............1889
†Welles, Mrs. John...........1902
†Welsh, Osgood..............1881
†Wendell, Evert Jansen........1900
Werner, Adolph..............1865

†Wesley, Edward B. 1857
Weston, Lillian R. 1902
†Wetmore, Charles H. 1858
†Wetmore, George Peabody. . . .1875
†Wheeler, Everett P. 1863
†Whitaker, Rev. Arthur. 1886
Whitaker, John E. 1902
†White, Alain C. 1903
White, John Jay, jr. 1902
°†White, Mrs. Joseph M. 1902
†White, Wm. Augustus. 1857
†Whitlock, Bache McEvers. . . .1879
Whitman, Charles Seymour. . . .1903
†Whitney, Charles A. 1886
Whitridge, Frederick W. 1886
†Whittaker, Thomas. 1879
Wicker, Cassius M. 1902
Wiener, Frank. 1896
†Wilder, Louis D. V., M.D. 1864
Wilkins, Rev. Gouverneur Morris. 1892
†Wilkinson, James. 1887
†Willcox, David. 1901
†Willets, John T. 1886
†Williams, Benjamin C. 1902
†Williams, David. 1882
Wills, Charles T. 1902
†Wilson, George. 1883
Wilson, Henry R. 1902
†Wilson, M. Orme. 1902
†Windmuller, Louis. 1891
†Winthrop, Benjamin R. 1857
†Winthrop, Egerton Leigh. 1857
†Winthrop, Grenville L. 1893
†Winthrop, William Neilson. . . .1857
†Witthaus, Rudolph A., M.D. . .1862
†Wood, Arthur King. 1901
†Wood, Charles F. 1892
†Wood, Mrs. Isaac F. 1878
†Wood, William H. S. 1889
†Woodruff, Baker. 1857
†Woodruff, Francis E. 1898
Woolsey, Theodorus B. 1870
†Wright, John M. 1857
†Wyckoff, William F. 1901
†Wysong, John J. 1902

†Young, William Hopkins. 1896
†York, Edward Palmer. 1902

†Zabriskie, Andrew C. 1881

Note.—In the preceding list, a dagger (†) before the name indicates a Life Member, * Patron, ° Fellow.

SUBSCRIBERS.

SUBSCRIBERS TO THE FUND FOR THE PURCHASE OF SITE FOR NEW BUILDING

CENTRAL PARK WEST

SEVENTY-SIXTH TO SEVENTY-SEVENTH STREETS.

Mrs. Robert L. Stuart	$100,000 00
John S. Kennedy	15,000 00
George W. Vanderbilt	15,000 00
J. Pierpont Morgan	10,000 00
Cornelius Vanderbilt	10,000 00
Miss Catherine Wolfe Bruce	10,000 00
Miss Matilda Wolfe Bruce	10,000 00
John Alsop King	8,500 00
Alfred Corning Clark	7,200 00
John Divine Jones	5,000 00
Mrs. Augustus Schell	5,000 00
Miss Charlotte A. Mount	2,500 00
Miss Susan Mount	2,500 00
William K. Vanderbilt	2,000 00
Robert Schell	2,000 00
Benjamin H. Field	1,500 00
Henry Herrman	1,000 00
Mrs. Henry Herrman	1,000 00
David Dows	1,000 00
William Waldorf Astor	1,000 00
Collis P. Huntington	1,000 00
Henry G. Marquand	1,000 00
Goldsborough Banyer	1,000 00
Ambrose K. Ely	1,000 00
Phillips Phoenix	1,000 00
Lloyd Phoenix	1,000 00
W. Bayard Cutting	1,000 00
R. Fulton Cutting	1,000 00
Miss Julia Rhinelander	1,000 00
Miss Serena Rhinelander	1,000 00
Robert J. Livingston	1,000 00
Darius O. Mills	1,000 00

William H. Jackson	$1,000 00
Charles Lanier	1,000 00
James M. Constable	1,000 00
Robert Winthrop	1,000 00
Percy R. Pyne	1,000 00
Frederick Billings	1,000 00
Cornelius N. Bliss	1,000 00
Gerard Beekman	1,000 00
Daniel Parish, jr.	1,000 00
John A. Weekes	1,000 00
Franklin H. Delano	1,000 00
Adrian Iselin	1,000 00
Frederick Sturges	1,000 00
Charles L. Tiffany	1,000 00
William C. Schermerhorn	1,000 00
William Austin	1,000 00
William L. Skidmore	1,000 00
Samuel D. Babcock	1,000 00
William D. Sloane	1,000 00
Mrs. Charles H. Rogers	1,000 00
William B. Isham	1,000 00
Abram Dubois, M.D	1,000 00
David Stewart	1,000 00
Miss Rachel L. Kennedy	1,000 00
Harris C. Fahnestock	1,000 00
Levi P. Morton	1,000 00
George Bliss	1,000 00
Daniel B. Fayerweather	1,000 00
Woodbury G. Langdon	1,000 00
Orlando B. Potter	1,000 00
Martin E. Greene	1,000 00
Samuel Riker	900 00
Albert R. Gallatin	500 00
Miss Mary L. Kennedy	500 00
William Astor	500 00
Thomas N. Lawrence	500 00
Mrs. Sarah J. Zabriskie	500 00
Morris K. Jesup	500 00
Frederick F. Thompson	500 00
George G. Williams	500 00
Elliott F. Shepard	500 00
J. Hampden Robb	500 00
Isaac J. Greenwood	500 00
Mary Greenwood	500 00
Andrew C. Zabriskie	500 00

Edward F. de Lancey	$500 00
Mrs. William H. Osborn	500 00
Richard T. Auchmuty	500 00
William M. Evarts	500 00
Henry Dexter	500 00
A. Van Horne Stuyvesant	250 00
Charles Howland Russell	250 00
Maturin L. Delafield	250 00
Mrs. Jonathan Sturges	250 00
George Peabody Wetmore	250 00
Mrs. Frank W. Jackson	250 00
Amos R. Eno	250 00
Josiah M. Fiske	250 00
Frederic Bronson	250 00
John L. Riker	200 00
Herman C. van Post	200 00
William Remsen	200 00
Jacob Wendell	200 00
George F. Baker	200 00
James C. Carter	200 00
Hugh N. Camp	200 00
Charles W. Sloane	200 00
Elbridge T. Gerry	100 00
Stuyvesant Fish	100 00
John H. Riker	100 00
William T. Buckley	100 00
Jenkins Van Schaick	100 00
Rev. Samuel M. Jackson	100 00
Samuel Sloan	100 00
Charles G. Langdon	100 00
James W. Gerard	100 00
Frederick B. Jennings	100 00
Mrs. James A. Glover	100 00
John Bigelow	100 00
Robert Halstead	100 00
William Lummis	100 00
Edward N. Dickerson	100 00
Henry T. Drowne	100 00
Robert Harris	100 00
Hicks Arnold	100 00
Orlando M. Harper	100 00
Charles A. Peabody	100 00
James D. Lynch	100 00
John T. Agnew	100 00
John A. Hadden	100 00

Henry Clews	$100 00
Morgan Dix, D.D	100 00
James A. Garland	100 00
James Talcott	100 00
Charles F. Southmayd	100 00
Rev. Richard L. Burtsell	100 00
Hiram Hitchcock	100 00
Robert Ray Hamilton	100 00
Abram S. Hewitt	100 00
Albert L. Loomis, M.D	100 00
Henry C. Sturges	100 00
W. Seward Webb, M.D	100 00
Walter Langdon	100 00
Franklin Burdge	100 00
Woolsey R. Hopkins	100 00
John McKesson, jr.	100 00
Henry Dudley	100 00
Jonathan H. Crane	100 00
Elihu Chauncey	50 00
Henry E. Lawrence	50 00
Oliver G. Barton	50 00
John T. Lockman	50 00
Hamilton B. Tompkins	50 00
John Clinton Gray	50 00
William Augustus White	50 00
Thomas C. Wood	50 00
Robert Goelet	25 00
Ogden Goelet	25 00
Henry E. Gregory	25 00
Charles E. Strong	25 00
Edgar M. Crawford	25 00
John S. Craig	25 00
Lazarus Rosenfeld	25 00
Addison Brown	25 00
Richard J. Leggat	25 00
George Wilson	25 00

SUBSCRIBERS TO THE BUILDING FUND.

Legacy of Robert Schell	$23,812 50
Archer Milton Huntington	20,000 00
Miss Matilda Wolfe Bruce	15,000 00
The Very Reverend Eugene Augustus Hoffman, D.D	10,000 00
F. Robert Schell	10,000 00
"A Friend of the Society" (through Gouverneur Tillotson)	10,000 00
"A Friend of the Society" (through Samuel Thorne)	10,000 00
Samuel Verplanck Hoffman	5,500 00
John Alsop King	5,000 00
Miss Charlotte A. Mount	5,000 00
Miss Susan Mount	5,000 00
Charles A. Sherman (in memory of Charles P. Huntington)	5,000 00
Mrs. Frederick F. Thompson	5,000 00
William C. Schermerhorn	5,000 00
Mrs. Eugene Augustus Hoffman	2,000 00
Miss Phebe Anne Thorne	1,000 00
Miss Mary Rhinelander King	1,000 00
Miss Serena Rhinelander	1,000 00
Edward S. Clark	1,000 00
Daniel Parish, jr.	1,000 00
Mrs. Richard T. Auchmuty	1,000 00
Herman C. von Post	1,000 00
Theodore F. Jackson	1,000 00
Isaac J. Greenwood	1,000 00
Mrs. James M. Lawton	1,000 00
Miss Caroline Phelps Stokes	1,000 00
Nicholas Fish	1,000 00
Charles A. Hoyt	1,000 00
Mrs. Charles Frederick Hoffman	1,000 00
Frederic Wendell Jackson	1,000 00
Henry Phipps	1,000 00
George G. Williams	1,000 00
William K. Vanderbilt	1,000 00
James Speyer	1,000 00
Mrs. Joseph M. White	1,000 00
Samuel Sloan	1,000 00
Frank Tilford	1,000 00
Mrs. Henry Herrman	1,000 00

Henry H. Cook	$1,000 00
George F. Baker	1,000 00
Harris C. Fahnestock	1,000 00
Mrs. Morris K. Jesup	1,000 00
Mrs. John E. Parsons	1,000 00
Murray Guggenheim	500 00
John C. Osgood	500 00
John E. Parsons	500 00
Frederick Billings	500 00
Mrs. J. Henry Watson	500 00
Mrs. Thomas W. Nickerson, jr.	500 00
Mrs. Charles L. Hackstaff	500 00
Mrs. Daniel M. Stimson	300 00
Sidney Webster	250 00
Mrs. J. Herman Aldrich	250 00
Stuyvesant Fish	250 00
John C. Havemeyer	200 00
William Alexander Smith	100 00
Marinus W. Dominick	100 00
James J. Higginson	100 00
Mrs. Cornelius Vanderbilt	100 00
Woodbury G. Langdon	100 00
Anson Phelps Stokes	100 00
Nathaniel W. Hunt	100 00
A. Lanfear Norrie	50 00
Addison Brown	50 00
Frederic J. de Peyster	50 00
George Abeel	25 00
Mrs. Eugenia Brodhead	25 00
Wm. R. Huntington, D.D.	25 00
Abram S. Post	25 00
Evert Jansen Wendell	25 00
Francis E. Woodruff	25 00
Mrs. Frederick Hasbrouck	25 00
Jacob Rothschild	20 00
J. Marcus Boorman	20 00
Samuel Sherwood	15 00
Miss Mary F. Hall	10 00
John Neilson Beekman, M.D.	10 00
Thomas Gallaudet, D.D.	10 00
Wm. Gray Schauffler, M.D.	5 00
Cash	1 00

Henry Dexter, for erection of Memorial Building	250,000 00

FUNDS.

PERMANENT FUNDS.

THE ISAIAH THOMAS FUND.—The legacy of Isaiah Thomas, of Worcester, Mass., in 1832, $300.

THE ELIZABETH DEMILT FUND.—The legacy of Miss Elizabeth Demilt, of New York, in 1849, $5,000.

THE SETH GROSVENOR FUND.—The legacy of Seth Grosvenor, of New York, in 1858, $10,000.

THE DAVID E. WHEELER FUND.—The legacy of David E. Wheeler, of New York, in 1870, $1,000.

THE THOMAS BARRON FUND.—The legacy of Thomas Barron, of New York, in 1875, $10,000.

THE RICHARD E. MOUNT FUND.—The legacy of Richard E. Mount, of New York, in 1880, $1,000.

THE EDWARD BILL FUND.—The legacy of Edward Bill, of New York, in 1884, $5,000.

THE AUGUSTUS SCHELL FUND.—The legacy of Augustus Schell, of New York, in 1884, $5,000.

THE MARY ROGERS FUND.—The legacy of Mrs. Charles H. Rogers, of New York, in 1891, $1,000.

THE JAMES FRANCIS EVANS FUND.—The legacy of Captain James Francis Evans, of New York, in 1893, $1,000.

THE HENRY KETELTAS FUND.—The legacy of Henry Keteltas, of New York, in 1898, $5,000.

THE CHARLES P. DALY FUND.—The legacy of Charles P. Daly, of New York, in 1900, $5,000.

THE MARIA BRANSON MOUNT FUND.—The legacy of Miss Maria Branson Mount, of New York, in 1901, $1,000.

THE EUGENE AUGUSTUS HOFFMAN MEMORIAL FUND.—The legacy of Dean Hoffman, 1902, late President of the Society, $50,000.

SPECIAL FUNDS.

THE PUBLICATION FUND.—Established by the Society in 1858, for the Publication of its Proceedings and Collections. Of the shares of the capital stock of this Fund, limited in number to 1,000, 829 have been sold up to the present time, as follows: 750 shares were sold prior to June 6, 1866, at $25 per share; subsequently the price of shares was advanced to $50, when thirty shares were sold at the latter figure; the price of shares was again advanced, January 1, 1883, to $100 per share, since then forty-six shares have been sold, realizing $25,150, the interest of which is used for the publication of each successive volume. Thirty volumes have been published, 1868–1897.

THE FUND OF THE SONS OF RHODE ISLAND.—The gift of the Association in New York known by that name during the Civil War, presented in 1866, and devoted to the purchase of works for the Library relating to the history of Rhode Island, $600.

THE JOHN DIVINE JONES FUND.—Founded by John Divine Jones, of New York, in 1879, for the publication and sale by the Society of works relating to the early history of New York and other American Provinces. This fund now amounts to $4,416.55. The History of New York during the Revolutionary War. By Thomas Jones. Edited by Edward F. de Lancey. 2 volumes. 8vo. New York, 1879, have been published.

THE STEPHEN WHITNEY PHŒNIX FUND.—The bequest of Stephen Whitney Phœnix, of New York, in 1882, for the maintenance and increase of the Phœnix Collection of Heraldry and Genealogy, $15,000.

BUILDING FUND

Balance on hand.................... $85,396.74

TRUSTEES OF THE NEW BUILDING.

Henry Dexter gift....................$250,000.00

BIBLIOGRAPHY.

BIBLIOGRAPHY.

Address to the Public, February 12, 1805. 4to, pp. 4.

Constitution and by-laws. Instituted the 10th of December, 1804. 8vo, pp. 15. New York, 1805.

Address to the Public, September 15, 1809. Broadside.

First celebration of the festival of St. Nicholas by the Society, December 6, 1810. Broadside.

A discourse designed to commemorate the discovery of New York by Henry Hudson; delivered before the Society, September 4, 1809, being the completion of the second century since that event. By Samuel Miller, D.D. 8vo, pp. 28. New York, 1810.

Anniversary discourse before the Society, December 6, 1811. By De Witt Clinton. 8vo, pp. 81 (1). New York, 1812.

New York Historical Society. Collections. Vols. I–V; second series, Vols. I–IV. 8vo. New York, 1811–1859.

CONTENTS.

Vol. I. Collections for 1809: Constitution; Discourse, designed to commemorate the discovery of New York by Henry Hudson, September 4, 1809, by Samuel Miller; Divers voyages and Northern discoveries of Henry Hudson, 1607; A second voyage of Henry Hudson, 1608; The third voyage of Henry Hudson, 1609; An abstract of the journal of Henry Hudson, 1610; Documents concerning the early history of New York, from Hazard's "Historical Collections"; Laws established by James, Duke of York, for the government of New York in 1664. 8vo, pp. vi, 428. New York, 1811.

Vol. II. Collections for 1814: Preface; Memorial to the legislature; Members; Officers; A discourse on the benefits of civil history, before the Society, December 6, 1810, by Hugh Williamson; A discourse before the Society at their anniversary meeting, December 6, 1811, by De Witt Clinton [on the Indians of New York]; A discourse before the Society, December 6, 1812, by Gouverneur Morris ["on some prominent historical facts and circumstances which distinguish our State"]; A discourse before the Society, December 6, 1813, embracing a concise and comprehensive account of the writings which illustrate the botanical history of North and South America, by Samuel L. Mitchill; An account of De La

Salle's last expedition and discoveries in North America [on the Mississippi], by H. Tonti; An extract of a translation of the history of New Sweed Land in America, by Thomas Companius Holm, 1703; Catalogue of the books, tracts, newspapers, maps, charts, views, portraits, and manuscripts in the library of the Society. New York, December 22, 1813. 8vo, pp. (4), xxii, (2), 23–358; (4), 139. New York, 1814.

Vol. III. Collections for 1821: Members; Officers; Inaugural discourse by Gouverneur Morris, September 4, 1816; Anniversary discourse before the Society, December 7, 1818, by Gulian C. Verplanck; A biographical memoir of Hugh Williamson, November 1, 1819, by David Hosack; A discourse on the religion of the Indian tribes of North America, December 20, 1819, by Samuel Farmar Jarvis; an inaugural address, second Tuesday of February, 1820, by David Hosack; An anniversary discourse, December 28, 1820, by Henry Wheaton [on the history of the science of public or international law]; Notes on a pamphlet entitled "A discourse before the New York Historical Society, December 6, 1811," by Samuel Jones; An extract from the records in the Council Chamber, relative to the dispute between the government of New Netherlands and the Lord Proprietary of Maryland, concerning the title of the Dutch to the territories on the Delaware, 1656–1668; Description of some of the medals struck in relation to important events in North America, before and since the Declaration of Independence, by James Mease. 8vo, pp. 404. Portrait. New York, 1821.

Vol. IV. (1826.) Continuation of Smith's History of New York. 8vo, pp. (8), 308. New York, 1826. (Reprinted in 1829 as Vol. V.)

Vol. IV. (1829.) History of the late province of New York from its discovery to the appointment of Governor Colden, in 1762. By the late Hon. William Smith. 8vo, pp. xvi, 320. New York, 1829. Pages ix–xvi contain memoir of William Smith, by his son. This is a revised edition of Smith's History as published at London, 1757.

Vol. V. The history of the province of New York, from its discovery to the appointment of Governor Colden. 8vo, pp. (6), 308. New York, 1829.

This is a reprint of Vol. IV (1826). The object of the reprinting of this continuation was to supply a complete edition of Smith's History, which was done by reprinting the original work as Vol. I and the continuation as Vol. II (IV and V of the *Collections*).

Second series, Vol. I. Anniversary discourse, by James Kent, December 6, 1828 [on the domestic history of the State (New York)]; Voyage of Verazzano along the coast of North America, 1524, translated by J. G. Cogswell; Indian tradition of the first arrival of the Dutch at Manhattan Island; A history of the New Netherlands, by Sir N. C. Lambrechtsen; translated by F. A. Van der Kemp; Description of the New Netherlands, by A. Van der Donck, translated by J. Johnson; Extracts from the voyages of David Pieterzen de Vries, translated by

G. Troost; Extracts from the New World, or a description of the West Indies, by John de Laet, translated by George Folsom; Extracts from the journal of the *Half-moon*, Henry Hudson, master, to the coast of America in 1609, by Robert Juet; Expedition of Capt. Samuel Argall to the French settlements in Acadia and Manhattan Island, 1613, by George Folsom; Letter of Thomas Dermer, describing his passage from Maine to Virginia, 1619; Correspondence between the colonies of New Netherlands and New Plymouth, 1627; The charter of liberties, 1629; A catalogue of the members of the Dutch Church, with the names of the streets of New York, 1686; New Sweden, or the Swedish settlements on the Delaware, by I. Acrelius; Report of Andreas Hudde [on the Swedes on the Delaware], 1645; Governor Rising's official report concerning the invasion of the Swedish colony in Nova Svecia, by the Dutch, 1655; The directors-general or governors of New Netherlands, by George Folsom; Historical sketch of the New York Historical Society, by George Folsom; Officers of the Society, 1805–1841; Members; Index. 8vo, pp. 486 (1). Folded map. Portrait. Plate. New York, 1841.

Second series, Vol. II. Officers; Outline of the constitutional history of New York, an anniversary discourse, November 19, 1847, by Benjamin Franklin Butler; Memoir read December 31, 1816 [on names of places in Dutch New York], by Egbert Benson; Narrative of the expedition of the Marquis De Nonville against the Senecas, in 1687, translated from the French, with notes, by O. H. Marshall; Correspondence between Lieutenant-Governor Cadwallader Colden and William Smith, jr., the historian, respecting certain alleged errors in the history of New York; Letter from Edmund Burke, respecting the effect of the Quebec bill upon the boundary of New York; Remarks upon the British expedition to Danbury, Conn., in 1777, by E. D. Whittlesey; New York in 1692, letter from Charles Lodwick; The representation of New Netherlands, concerning its location, productiveness, and poor condition, translated from the Dutch [of A. Van der Donck] by Henry C. Murphy; New Netherlands in 1627; Letter from I. de Rasieres, translated by J. Romeyn Brodhead; Memoir of the early colonization of New Netherland, by J. Romeyn Brodhead; Hudson's voyage in 1609, Extract from "Verhael von de eerste Schip-vaert der Hollandische . . . door 't Way-Gat by Noorden, . . . na Cathay ende China, voor Joost Hartgers," translated by J. Romeyn Brodhead; Extract from De Laet and Aitzema, relating to New Netherland; History of the New York Chamber of Commerce, with notices of some of its distinguished members, by Charles King; Table of the killed and wounded in the war of 1812, compiled by William Jay; Memoir of Theophilus Eaton, the first governor of the colony of New Haven, by Jacob Bailey Moore. 8vo, pp. vi, (2), 493. New York, 1849.

Second series, Vol. III, part 1. Voyages from Holland to America, 1612–1644, by D. P. De Vries, translated by Henry C. Murphy; Short sketch of the Mohawk Indians in New Netherland, etc., by J. Megapolensis, jr.; translation revised with an introduction by J. Romeyn Brodhead; The Jogues papers, translated and arranged by John Gilmary Shea; Extracts from Castell's Discovery of America, 1644; Broad advice to the untied Netherland provinces, translated from the Dutch, by Henry C. Murphy; Extract from Wagenaar's Beschryving van Amsterdam, relating to the colony of New Amstel (Newcastle), translated by J. Romeyn Brodhead; The seven articles from the church of Leyden, 1617, communicated by George Bancroft; Journal of an embassy from Canada to the united colonies of New England, in 1650, by Father Gabriel Druillettes, translated by John Gilmary Shea; Proceedings of the first assembly of Virginia, 1619, communicated, with an introductory note, by George Bancroft. 8vo, pp. iv, (4), 358 (1). New York, 1857.

The second part of this volume, which was to have contained "The Duke of York's charters of liberties and privileges to the inhabitants of New York, anno 1683," was never published.

Second series, Vol. IV. Catalogue of the Library of the Society. 8vo, pp. viii, 653. New York, 1859.

Discourse before the Society, at their anniversary meeting, December 6, 1812. By Gouverneur Morris. 8vo, pp. 40. New York, 1813.

Catalogue of the books, tracts, newspapers, maps, charts, views, portraits, and manuscripts in the library. 8vo, pp. (2) 2, 9–139. New York, 1813.

Memorial of the Society to the legislature of New York. 8vo, pp. 11. New York, 1814.

A catalogue of the resident and honorary members of the Society. 8vo, pp. 12 (2). New York, 1814.

Inaugural discourse before the Society, by Gouverneur Morris, September 4, 1816; the two hundred and sixth anniversary of the discovery of New York by Hudson. 8vo, pp. 24. New York, 1816.

Memoir read before the Historical Society of the State of New York, December 31, 1816. By Egbert Benson. 12mo, pp. 72. Jamaica, 1816.

Memoir read before the Historical Society of the State of New York, December 31, 1816. By Egbert Benson. 8vo, pp. 72. New York, 1817.

Same. Second edition, with notes. 12mo, pp. 127. Jamaica, 1825.

Memoir read before the Historical Society of the State of New York, December 31, 1816. By Egbert Benson. Reprinted from a copy with the author's last corrections. 8vo, pp. 72. New York, 1848.

Circular of the Mineralogical Committee, March 11, 1817. 4to, pp. 2.

Circular. American zoology and geology. 4to, pp. 2. New York, March 11, 1817.

Report on botany and vegetable physiology read at a meeting of the Society, April 8, 1817. Broadside.

Circular of Committee on Botany, April 8, 1817. 4to sheet, one page.

Directions to be observed in collecting and preserving Plants, April 8, 1817. Broadside.

Circular letter of the Committee for collecting manuscripts and scarce books. New York, March, 1817. 4to sheet, one page.

An anniversary discourse before the Society, December 7, 1818. By Gulian C. Verplanck. 8vo, pp. (2), 121. New York, 1818.

Same. 8vo, pp. 101. New York, 1821.

A history of the introduction and use of Scutellaria Lateriflora (Scullcap) as a remedy for preventing and curing hydrophobia, occasioned by the bite of rabid animals; with cases. Accompanied with a plate of the plant. By Lyman Spalding, M.D. Read before the New York Historical Society, September 14, 1819. 8vo, pp. 30. New York, 1819.

A biographical memoir of Hugh Williamson. Delivered on the 1st of November, 1819, at the request of the Society. By David Hosack. 8vo, pp. 91. New York, 1820.

Same. 8vo, pp. 78. New York, 1821.

A discourse on the religion of the Indian tribes of North America. Delivered before the Society, December 20, 1819. By Samuel Farmar Jarvis. 8vo, pp. 111. New York, 1820.

Inaugural address before the Society, February 2, 1820. By David Hosack. 8vo, pp. 14. New York, 1820.

Procès verbal of the ceremony of installation of president [David Hosack] of the Society as it will be performed February 8, 1820. [By Gulien C. Verplanck.] 8vo, pp. 18. New York, 1820.

A burlesque. Reprinted 1864. pp. 13 (2). Thirty-five copies.

An anniversary discourse before the Society, December 28, 1820. By Henry Wheaton. 8vo, pp. 49. New York, 1821.

A biographical memoir of Samuel Bard, M.D., LL.D., late President of the College of Physicians and Surgeons of the University of the State of New York, etc. With a critique upon his writings. Read before the Society, August 14, 1821. By Henry William Ducachet, M.D. 8vo, pp. 27. From the 4th volume of the American Recorder, October, 1821. Philadelphia.

Anniversary discourse before the Society, December 6, 1823, by William Sampson, showing the origin, progress, antiquities, curiosities, and nature of the common law. 8vo, pp. 68. New York, 1824.

Memorial to the legislature of the State of New York. List of officers and members. 8vo, pp. 32. New York, 1827.

An anniversary discourse before the Society, December 13, 1827. By Joseph Blunt. 8vo, pp. 52. New York, 1828.

An anniversary discourse before the Society, December 6, 1828. By James Kent. 8vo, pp. 40. New York, 1829.

Circular addressed to the members by the Treasurer, October, 1828. 4to sheet, one page.

Constitution and by-laws. 12mo, pp. 21. New York, 1829.

The origin and nature of the representative institutions of the United States; an anniversary discourse, before the Society, on the 19th of April, 1832. By William Beach Lawrence. 8vo, pp. 44. New York, 1832.

Catalogue, with history of the Society. New York, 1838.

Constitution and by-laws. 8vo, pp. 23. New York, 1839.

The jubilee of the Constitution. A discourse delivered at the request of the Society on the 30th of April, 1839, being the fiftieth anniversary of the inauguration of George Washington as President of the United States, the 30th of April, 1789. By John Quincy Adams. 8vo, pp. 136. Plate. New York, 1839.

Menu. Semi-centennial anniversary festival of the inauguration of George Washington as President of the United States, April 30, 1839. Broadside.

Address before the Society, 1839. [By Joseph Blunt.] (In his speeches, reviews, reports, etc. 8vo, pp. 151–195. New York, 1843.)

Lecture on the life and military services of Gen. James Clinton. Read before the Society, February 12, 1839. By William W. Campbell. 8vo, pp. 23. New York, 1839.

Catalogue of books, manuscripts, maps, etc., added to the library since January 19, 1839. 8vo, pp. 32. New York, 1840.

"The infancy of the Union." A discourse delivered before the Society, December 19, 1839. By William B. Reed. 8vo, pp. 50 (2). Philadelphia, 1840.

A description of New Netherlands (as the same are at the present time); comprehending the fruitfulness and natural advantages of the country and the desirable opportunities which it presents, within itself, and from abroad for the subsistence of man; which are not surpassed elsewhere. . . . With a dialogue between a Netherland patriot and a New Netherlander on the advantages of the country. Written by Adrian Van der Donck.

[Translated by J. Johnson.] The second edition, with a map of the country. At Amsterdam, published by Evert Nieuwenhof, bookseller, A.D. 1650. 8vo. New York. Reprinted, 1841.

From the *Collections*, No. 2.

Inaugural address of the Hon. Albert Gallatin on taking the chair as president of the Society, February 7, 1843. 8vo, pp. 21 (1). New York, 1843.

A memoir on the Northeastern boundary, in connection with Mr. Jay's map, by Albert Gallatin; together with a speech on the same subject, by Daniel Webster, delivered at a special meeting of the Society, April 15, 1843. Illustrated by a copy of the "Jay map." 8vo, pp. (2), 74. New York, 1843.

Constitution and by-laws. 8vo, pp. 33. New York, 1844.

An address before the Society at its fortieth anniversary, November 20, 1844; by John Romeyn Brodhead. With an account of the subsequent proceedings at the dinner. 8vo, pp. 107. New York, 1844.

Proceedings, seven volumes. 8vo. New York, 1844–1859.

1843. Annual report; Proceedings on the death of Peter A. Jay; Progress of ethnology, by John R. Bartlett; Notice of a military journal of the French and Indian war, by H. Schoolcraft; Paper on the "distinctive character of the people of New York," by C. F. Hoffman; Proceedings on the decease of Colonel Trumbull. 8vo, pp. 154. New York, 1844.

1844. Annual report; New Netherland, by Rev. Dr. De Witt; Ancient Indian stocks of North America, east of the Mississippi, by H. R. Schoolcraft; Some passages in the life of Governor Tompkins; The romance of American history (poem), by Thomas Ward. 8vo, pp. 213. New York, 1845.

1845. Annual report; Sketches of biographical writers and their works of the State of New York, by William L. Stone; The Indian names of Long Island, by B. F. Thompson; Historical considerations, on the siege and defence of Fort Stanwix, in 1776, by H. R. Schoolcraft; The direct agency of the English Government in the employment of the Indians in the Revolutionary war, by W. W. Campbell; Memoir of Samuel Osgood, by Osgood Field; Observations respecting the two ancient maps of New Netherland, found in the royal archives at the Hague, in 1841, by J. Romeyn Brodhead. 8vo, pp. 229. New York. 1846.

1846. Annual report; Memorial to the Legislature; Memoir of the French and Indian expedition against New York, which surprised and burned Schenectady, February 9, 1689–1690, by Maunsell Van Rensselaer; Notices of some antique earthen vessels found in the low tumuli of Florida [etc.], by H. R. Schoolcraft; Observations to show that the Grand Turk Island, and not San Salvador, was the first spot on which Columbus landed in the New World, by George Gibbs; The progress of geography and ethnology, by J. R. Bartlett. 8vo, pp. 214. Two plates. New York, 1847.

1847. Annual meeting; History of the Federal seat of government, by J. B. Varnum; "Defeat of General St. Clair in 1791," by C. R. Gilman; "Early European colonies on the Delaware," by J. W. Beekman; "The battle of Ticonderoga, 1758," by B. F. Thompson; Jesuit relations and discoveries, and other occurrences in Canada and the Northern and Western States, 1632–1672, by E. B. O'Callaghan. 8vo, pp. (8), 174. New York, 1847.

1848. Officers; Annual election; Reports; Proceedings on death of Chancellor Kent; "On the sources of some of the early settlements in the State of New York," by Rev. Dr. De Witt; "On proposed amendments to the Constitution of the United States, with original unpublished letters from distinguished statesmen," by J. H. Raymond; Translation of a letter of I. de Rasiere, in 1627, giving an account of New Netherland;

Notes from "Wassenaer's Historische Verhael"; "Fénélon among the Iroquois," by Robert Greenhow. (Greenhow's paper was issued as a supplement.) 8vo, pp. viii, 5–209. New York, 1849.

1849. Officers; Annual election; Report upon the aborginal monuments of western New York, by E. G. Squier; Notes for a memoir of Peter Minuit, by George H. Moore; Champlain in the Onondaga Valley, by O. H. Marshall; The ancient architecture of America, by R. C. Long; Our Dutch progenitors, by J. W. Knevels; History of religious missions, by J. W. Beekman; Reminiscences of Albert Gallatin, by J. R. Bartlett. 8vo, pp. 298. Plates. New York, 1849.

Debate in the Society on "Columbia" as the new name of this country, instead of "America," May 15, 1845. 8vo. New York, 1845.

Report of the aborginal names and geographical terminology of the State of New York. Part 1. Valley of the Hudson. Made to the Society by the committee appointed to prepare a map, etc., and read at the stated meeting of the Society, February, 1844. By Henry R. Schoolcraft. Published from the Society's *Proceedings* for 1844. 8vo, pp. 43. New York, 1845.

The imprint reads in some copies "Printed for the Society"; in others "Printed for the Author."

Report of the committee of the Society on a national name, March 31, 1845. 8vo, pp. 8. No title-page. New York, 1845.

A discourse delivered before the Society, at its forty-first anniversary, November, 20, 1845. By Alexander W. Bradford. 8vo, pp. 31. New York, 1846.

Historical considerations on the siege and defence of Fort Stanwix in 1777. Read before the Society, June 19, 1845. By Henry R. Schoolcraft. 8vo, pp. 29. New York, 1846.

The charter and by-laws. Revised March, 1846. 8vo, pp. 47. New York, 1846.

Notices of some antique earthen vessels, found in the low tumuli of Florida, and in the caves and burial places of the Indian tribes north of those latitudes. Read before the Society, June 2, 1846. 8vo, pp. 15. Plates. Reprinted from *Proceedings*. New York, 1847.

Incentives to the study of the ancient period of American history. An address delivered before the Society, at its forty-second anniversary, November 17, 1846. By Henry R. Schoolcraft. 8vo, pp. 38. New York, 1847.

Jesuit Relations of discoveries and other occurrences in Canada and the Northern and Western States of the Union. 1632–1672. By E. B. O'Callaghan. From the *Proceedings* of the Society. November, 1847. 8vo, pp. 22. New York, 1847.

The progress of ethnology; an account of recent archæological, philological, and geographical researches in various parts of the globe, tending to elucidate the physical history of man. By J. R. Bartlett. 8vo, pp. 151. New York, 1847.

The substance of this memoir was read before the New York Historical Society, and a portion before the American Ethnological Society.

Anniversary discourse, November 19, 1847. By Benjamin Franklin Butler. Outline of the constitutional history of New York. 8vo, pp. 75. New York, 1848.

Annual report of the Executive Committee for the year 1847. 8vo, pp. 15. New York, 1848.

Circular of Committee for procuring funds for the erection of building, October 30, 1848. 4to, pp. 3.

Historical and mythological traditions of the Algonquins; with a translation of the "Walum-Olum," or bark record of the Linni-Lenape. Read before the Society, June 5, 1848. 8vo, pp. 23.

In *American Review*, February, 1849.

History of the New York Chamber of Commerce, with notices of some of its most distinguished members. An anniversary discourse delivered before the Society, November 21, 1848. By Charles King. 8vo, pp. 66. New York, 1849.

Narrative of the expedition of the Marquis de Nonville against the Senecas, in 1687. Translated from the French, with an introductory notice and notes, by Orsamus H. Marshall. 8vo, pp. 48. Two maps. Reprinted from *Collections*. New York, 1848.

The ancient architecture of America. Discourse before the Society, April 3, 1849. By R. Cary Long. 8vo, pp. 37. Nine plates. New York, 1849.

By-laws of the committee or trustees of the building fund, 1850. 8vo, pp. 8. New York, 1850.

Antiquities of the State of New York. Illustrated by 14 quarto plates and 80 engravings on wood. By E. G. Squier. 8vo, pp. 343. Buffalo, 1851.

"The investigations, the results of which are embodied in the following pages were undertaken in the autumn of 1848, under the joint auspices of the Historical Society of New York and the Smithsonian Institution. They were originally, published in the second volume of the Smithsonian Contributions to Knowledge." (Preface.)

Letter to the trustees of the building fund of the Society. 8vo, pp. 21. New York, 1851.

An address delivered before the Society, February 23, 1852, by Daniel Webster. 8vo, pp. 57. New York, 1852.

Cotton. A paper on the growth, trade and manufacture of cotton. Read before the Society, March 2, 1852. By J. G. Dudley. 8vo, pp. 96. New York, 1853.

English colonization in America. A vindication of the claims of Sir Ferdinando Gorges as the father of English colonization in America. By J. A. Poor. Delivered before the historical societies of Maine and New York. 8vo, pp. 144. New York, 1852.

The Mecklenburg declaration of independence. A lecture by Francis L.

Hawks, delivered before the Society, at Metropolitan Hall, December 16, 1852. Woodcut. Folded plate of facsimiles.

In *Revolutionary History of North Carolina*, pp. 43–98. Raleigh, 1853. Compiled by W. D. Cooke.

The City of New York: Its growth, destinies and duties. A lecture delivered before the Society, January 6, 1853. By John A. Dix. 8vo, pp. 23. New York, 1853.

The discovery and colonization of America and immigration to the United States. A lecture delivered before the Society on the 1st of June, 1853. By Edward Everett. 8vo, pp. 32. Boston, 1853.

Address before the Society, by Edward Everett; with an introduction by J. R. Ingersoll. 8vo, pp. 40. London, 1853.

The charter and by-laws. Second edition, with amendments. 8vo, pp. 22. New York, 1853.

British invasion of North Carolina, in 1780 and 1781. A lecture by William A. Graham, delivered before the Society, in January, 1853. Woodcut.

In *Revolutionary History of North Carolina*. Compiled by W. D. Cooke. pp. 147–209. Raleigh, 1853.

Proceedings of the Society, October, 1853. Ruins of Tenampua, Honduras, Central America. [Letter from E. G. Squier, communicated by Prof. W. W. Turner, of Washington.] 12mo, pp. 8. [New York, 1853.]

Circular letter. September 12, 1854. 4to sheet, one page. New York, 1854.

The necessity, the realty, and the promise of the progress of the human race. Oration before the Society, November 20, 1854, by George Bancroft. 8vo, pp. 37. New York, 1854.

Semicentennial celebration. Fiftieth anniversary of the founding of the Society, November 20, 1854. 8vo, pp. 96. New York, 1854.

Semicentennial anniversary of the Society, November 20, 1854. List of Toasts. Broadside.

The seven articles from the Church of Leyden, 1617. With an introductory letter by George Bancroft. 8vo, pp. 10. [New York, 1856.]

From the *Collections of the Society*, second series, Vol. III.

Narrative of a captivity among the Mohawk Indians, a description of New Netherland in 1642–43, and other papers. By Isaac Jogues. With a memoir of the author by John Gilmary Shea. 8vo, pp. 69. New York, 1856.

Same, New York, 1857. 8vo, pp. 69.

Reprinted from the *Collections of the Society*.

A paper on the history and prospects of interoceanic communication by the American isthmus. Read by Lieut. I. C. [G.] Strain before the Society, June 17, 1856. 8vo, pp. 27. New York, 1856.

The Dutch at the north pole and the Dutch in Maine. A paper read before the Society, March 3, 1857. By J. Watts De Peyster. 8vo, pp. 80. New York, 1857.

Circular letter, January, 1857. [Erection of building.] 4to sheet, one page

Proceedings of the Society at the dedication of the library, November 3, 1857. 8vo, pp. 27. New York, 1857.

The Washington chair, presented to the Society by Benjamin Robert Winthrop, November 3, 1857. 8vo, pp. 10. Woodcut. New York [1857].

New York during the last half century; a discourse in commemoration of the fifty-third anniversary of the Society and of the dedication of their new edifice (November 17, 1857). By John W. Francis. 8vo, pp. 232. New York, 1857.

Old New York; or, reminiscences of the past sixty years. Being an enlarged and revised edition of the anniversary discourse delivered before the Society (November 17, 1857). By John W. Francis. 8vo, pp. 384. New York, 1858.

Proofs considered of the early settlement of Acadie by the Dutch, being an appendix to The Dutch in Maine. [By John Watts De Peyster.] 8vo, pp. 19. [New York, 1858.]

Catalogue of printed books in the library of the New York Historical Society. 8vo, pp. viii, 653. New York, 1859.

Henry Cruger, the colleague of Edmund Burke in the British Parliament. A paper read before the Society, January 4, 1859. By Henry C. Van Schaack. 8vo, pp. 67. New York, 1859.

Proceedings of the Society on the announcement of the death of W. H. Prescott, February, 1859. 8vo, pp. (2), 16. [New York, 1859.]

The Sons of Liberty in New York. A paper read before the Society, May 3, 1859. By Henry B. Dawson. 8vo, pp. 118. [New York] 1859.

Circular of Committee on purchase of the Egyptian Museum, May 14, 1859. 12mo, pp. 2.

"Mr. Lee's plan—March 29, 1777." The treason of Charles Lee, major-general, second in command in the American Army of the Revolution. By George H. Moore. Read before the Society, June 22, 1858. 8vo, pp. xii, 115 (1). Two portraits. Two folded sheets. New York, 1860.

Proceedings of the Society, December 6, 1859, on the death of Washington Irving. In *Irvingiana*. pp. 29–36. New York, 1860.

Discourse on the life, character, and genius of Washington Irving. Delivered before the Society on the 3d of April, 1860. By W. C. Bryant. 8vo, pp. 46. New York, 1860.

Circular. Purchase of the Egyptian collection, January 24, 1860. Single sheet, one page.

Declaration of Independence by the Colony of Massachusetts Bay, May 1, 1776. Letter to Luther Bradish, president of the Society. By Henry B. Dawson. January 7, 1862. 8vo, pp. 12. With facsimile. [New York, 1862.]

Annual report of the committee on the fine arts, January, 1862. 8vo, pp. 8. [New York, 1862.]

Old New York. Read before the Society, February 4, 1862, by Benjamin Robert Winthrop. 8vo, pp. 6. Map. New York, 1862.

Mr. Bancroft's letter on the exchange of prisoners during the American war of independence. February 14, 1862. 8vo, pp. 7, (4). [New York, 1862.]

Discourse on the life, character, and policy of Count Cavour, delivered in the hall of the Society, February 20, 1862. By Vincenzo Botta. 8vo, pp. 108. New York, 1862.

Sulla vita, natura e politica del Conte di Cavour, discorso di Vincenzo Botta nella Sala della Società storica di Nuova-York il 20 febbraio 1862. Versione dall' inglese [di Stanislao Gatti]. 8vo, pp. 98. Napoli, 1862.

The New York negro plot of 1741. A paper read before the Society, May 6, 1862. By John Gilmary Shea.

In *Manual of the Corporation of the City of New York*, 1870, pp. 764–771.

Catalogue of the museum and gallery of art of the Society. 8vo, pp. 72, 39. New York, 1862.

Charter and by-laws. Revised January, 1858; with a list of members. 8vo, pp. 73, (1). New York, 1862.

Treachery in Texas, the secession of Texas, and the arrest of the United States officers and soldiers serving in Texas. Read before the Society, June 25, 1861. By J. T. Sprague. 8vo, pp. 109–142. New York, 1862.

The life, writings, and character of Edward Robinson, D.D. Read before the Society, February 3 and March 24, 1863. By Henry B. Smith and Roswell D. Hitchcock. 12mo, pp. 100. New York, 1863.

The assault on Stony Point by Gen. Anthony Wayne, July 16, 1779. Prepared for the Society and read April 1, 1862. With maps, facsimiles, and illustrative notes. By H. B. Dawson. Large 8vo, pp. viii, 156. Morrisania, 1863.

Circular of committee on purchase of Audubon's original drawings of "The Birds of America." April 14, 1863. Single sheet, one page.

Address delivered at the celebration by the Society, May 20, 1863, of the two hundredth anniversary of the birthday of William Bradford, who introduced the art of printing into the middle colonies of British America, by John William Wallace. Published, with an introductory note, in pursuance of a resolution of the Society. 8vo, pp. 114. Albany, 1863.

When was the drama introduced in America? An historical inquiry anterior to Dunlap's History of the American theatre. Read before the Society. November 3, 1863. By Charles P. Daly. 8vo, pp. 12. New York, 1864,

The beginning of America. A discourse before the Society on its fifty-ninth anniversary, November 17, 1863, by Erastus C. Benedict. 8vo, pp. 64. New York, 1864.

An account of Abimelech Cordy and other celebrated writers of New York (thirty-five copies printed), 1864; procès verbal of the ceremony of installation of the president of the New York Historical Society. 8vo, pp. 2. New York, 1864.

A burlesque on the Society.

Circular to members. 1864. 8vo, pp. (4), 11, (1). [New York, 1864.]

List of officers. Revised, 1864.

Rules of the Executive Committee, 1864. 8vo, pp. 7. [New York, 1864.]

An inquiry into the authenticity of documents concerning a discovery in North America claimed to have been made by Verrazzano. Read before the Society, October 4, 1864. By Buckingham Smith. 8vo, pp. 31. Map. New York, 1864.

Commemoration of the conquest of New Netherland on its two hundredth anniversary, by the Society. 8vo, pp. 87. Map. New York, 1864.

Pages 5–58 are taken up with "Oration on the conquest of New Netherland, before the Society, the 12th of October, 1864. By John Romeyn Brodhead," with separate title-page.

Oration on the conquest of New Netherland. Delivered before the Society, October 12, 1863. By John Romeyn Brodhead. 8vo, pp. 54. Map. New York, 1864.

Procès verbal of the ceremony of installation of president of the New York Historical Society, as it will be performed February 8, 1820. 8vo, pp. 13, (2). Thirty-five copies. New York, 1820. Reprinted 1864.

Memoir of Rip Van Dam, by Frederic De Peyster. Read before the Society, November 4, 1862. 8vo, pp. 26. Two portraits. New York, 1865.

Proceedings of the Society on the death of Luther Bradish, president, October, 1863. 8vo, pp. 24, (2). Portrait. New York, 1865.

An address before the Society on its sixtieth anniversary, November 22, 1864. By Frederic De Peyster. 8vo, pp. (4), 76. Portrait. New York, 1865.

On the early political history of New York.

The annual discourse before the Society on the 20th of December, 1859. By George Folsom. 8vo, pp. 48. Ventnor, England, 1866.

The charter and by-laws. Revised January, 1858. With the amendments and a list of members. 8vo, pp. 38. New York, 1866.

Catalogue of the museum and gallery of art of the Society, 1866. 8vo, pp. viii, 72, 61, (1). New York, 1866.

The moral and intellectual influence of libraries upon social progress. An address before the Society on its sixty-first anniversary, November 21, 1865. By Frederic De Peyster. 8vo, pp. 96. New York, 1866.

Resident members of the Society, March, 1866. 8vo, pp. 16. [New York, 1866.]

North American rock-writing, and other aboriginal modes of recording and transmitting thought. By Thomas Ewbank. 8vo, pp. (3), 49. Morrisania, 1866.

Read before the Society, March 6, 1866, and published in the *Historical Magazine* for August, September, and October, 1866.

The government of Sir Edmond Andros over New England in 1688 and 1689. Read before the Society, December 4, 1866. By John Romeyn Brodhead. 8vo, pp. 40. Morrisania, N. Y., 1867.

New York in the nineteenth century. A discourse delivered before the Society on its sixty-second anniversary, November 20, 1866. By Samuel Osgood, D.D. 8vo, pp. 127. New York, 1867.

History and its philosophy. The address at the sixty-third anniversary of the Society, December 19, 1867. By C. S. Henry, D.D. 8vo, pp. 16. New York, 1868.

Catalogue of the museum and gallery of art of the Society, 1867. 8vo, viii, pp. 72, 61 (1). New York, 1867.

Collections. Vols. I–XXX. For the years 1868–1897. Publication fund series. New York, 1868–1898.

8vo. Thirty volumes.

CONTENTS.

Vol. I. 1868. Officers, 1868; The continuation of Chalmer's Political annals; Letters on Smith's History of New York, by Cadwallader Colden; Documents relating to the administration of Jacob Leisler. 8vo, pp. xviii, (2), 458. New York, 1869.

Vol. II. 1869. Officers, 1870; The Clarendon papers; Tracts relating to New York; The destruction of Schenectady; Arguments offered to the lords commissioners for trade and plantation relating to some acts of assembly passed at New York, in America, 1701; Miscellaneous documents; Letter of Cadwallader Colden on Smith's History, July 5, 1759; Documents concerning Plowden's New Albion; Notes and observations on the town of East Hampton, at the east end of Lond Island, written by John Lyon Gardiner, 1798; Notes and memorandums concerning Gardiners Island, written in May, 1798, by John Lyon Gardiner; Copy of James Farrett's grant to Lyon Gardiner; Note, witchcraft in New York; Collection of evidence in vindication of the territorial rights and jurisdiction of the State of New York against the claims of Massachusetts and New Hampshire and the people of the Grants, commcnly called Vermonters. 8vo, pp. xiv, (2), 560. New York, 1870.

Vol. III. 1870. Officers, 1871; State of the evidence and argument in support of the territorial rights and jurisdiction of New York against the government of New Hampshire, by James Duane; Old New York and Trinity church; Extracts from various newspapers, 1730–1785; Some remarks on the memorial and remonstrance of Trinity church, etc., 1785; Extracts from various newspapers, 1785–1790; A good conversation, a sermon preached at New York, January 19, 1706, by Francis Makemie. 8vo, pp. xii, (2), 488. New York, 1871.

Vol. IV. 1871. Officers, 1872; The Lee papers, Vol. I, 1751–1776. 8vo, pp. (10), 494. New York, 1872.

Vol. V. 1872. Officers, 1873; The Lee papers, Vol. II, 1776–1778. 8vo, pp. (8), 494. New York, 1873.

Vol. VI. 1873. Officers, 1874; The Lee papers, Vol. III, 1778–1782. 8vo, pp. (10), 494. New York, 1874.

Vol. VII. 1874. Officers of the Society, 1875; The Lee papers, Vol. IV, 1782–1811; Memoir of General Lee, by Isaac Langworthy, 1787; Memoir of General Lee, by Sir Henry Bunbury, Bart., 1838; Life of

Charles Lee, by Jared Sparks; The treason of Charles Lee, by George H. Moore. 8vo, pp. viii, (4), 500. New York, 1875.

Vol. VIII. 1875. Officers, 1876; Official letters of Maj. Gen. James Pattison, as commandant of the royal artillery in America [and] as commandant of the city of New York, 1779–80; Letters to Gen. Lewis Morris, 1775–1782. 8vo, pp. x, 33, (4), 553. New York, 1876.

Vol. IX. 1876. Officers, 1877; Introduction; The Colden letter books, Vol. I, 1760–1765; 1877. 8vo, pp. x, (2), 495. New York, 1877.

Vol. X. 1877. Officers, 1878; The Colden letter books, Vol. II, 1765–1775. 8vo, pp. (8), 531. New York, 1878.

Vol. XI. 1878. Officers, 1879; Revolutionary papers, Vol. I: The papers of Charles Thomson, secretary of the Continental Congress, 1765–1816; Correspondence; Debates in the Congress of the Confederation, July 22 to September 20, 1782; "Joseph Reed's narrative"; Letters of Colonel Armand (Marquis de la Rouerie), 1777–1791; Letters to Robert Morris, 1775–1782. 8vo, pp. xiv, (2), 503. New York, 1879.

Vol. XII. 1879. Officers, 1880; Revolutionary papers, Vol. II: The trial of Major-General Schuyler, October, 1778; The trial of Major-General Howe, December, 1781; Transactions as commissary for embarking foreign troops in the English service from Germany, 1776–1777, by Charles Rainsford. 8vo, pp. (10), 559. New York, 1880.

Vol. XIII. 1880. Officers, 1881; Revolutionary and miscellaneous papers, Vol. III.: Proceedings of a general court-martial for the trial of Major-General St. Clair, August 25, 1778; Journal of the most remarkable occurrences in Quebec, from the 14th of November, 1775, to the 7th of May, 1776, by an officer of the garrison; The case of William Atwood, 1703; A sermon preached in Trinity church, in New York, May 12, 1709, at the funeral of John, Lord Lovelace, by William Vesey; Rev. John Sharpe's "Proposals for erecting a school, library, and chapel at New York," 1712–1713; The first minister of the Reformed Protestant Dutch Church in America, letter of Domine Jonas Michaelius to Domine Adrianus Smoutius, dated at Manhattan, 11 August, 1628, translated from the Dutch, with a preface and notes, by Henry C. Murphy; Court of lieutenancy, 1686–1696; Index to Revolutionary and miscellaneous papers, Vols. I–III. 8vo, pp. xiii, (3), 489. Folded map. New York, 1881.

Vol. XIV. 1881. Officers, 1882; The Montrésor journals, edited and annotated by G. D. Scull; Family of Montrésor; Journals of Col. James Montrésor, 1757–1759; Journals of Capt. John Montrésor, 1757–1778; Appendix. 8vo, pp. xiv, 578. Portrait. Folded map. Plan. New York, 1882.

Vol. XV. 1882. Officers, 1883; Introduction; Biographical sketch of Lieutenant Von Krafft, with a prefatory note, by Thomas H. Edsall; Journal of Lieut. John Charles Philip von Krafft, of the regiment Von

Bose, 1776–1784; Letter book of Capt. Alexander McDonald, of the royal highland emigrants, 1775–1779; Index. 8vo, pp. xii, (4), 515. Four folded plates. New York, 1883.

Vol. XVI. 1883. Officers, 1884; Prefatory note; The Kemble papers, Vol. I, 1773–1789; Journals of Lieut. Col. Stephen Kemble, 1773–1789; Order books of Lieut. Col. Stephen Kemble, adjutant-general and deputy adjutant-general to the British forces in America, 1775–1778; Gen. Sir Henry Clinton's orders, 1778; Orders by Maj. Gen. Daniel Jones, commanding His Majesty's troops on New York Island and posts defending. 8vo, pp. xi, (5), 666. Portrait. New York, 1884.

Vol. XVII. 1884. Officers, 1885; Prefatory note; The Kemble papers, Vol. II, 1780–1781; Journals of Lieut. Col. Stephen Kemble, brigadier-general in command of the expedition to Nicaragua, 1780–1781; Orders of Brig. Gen. Stephen Kemble, expedition to Nicaragua, 1780–1781; Documents and correspondence; Expedition to the Spanish Main and Nicaragua, 1779–1781; Index to Kemble papers. 8vo, pp. xxiii, 472. Folded map. New York, 1885.

Vol. XVIII. 1885. Officers, 1886; The burghers of New Amsterdam and the freemen of New York, 1675–1866; The burgher right of New Amsterdam; Roll of freeman of New York City, 1675–1866; Indentures of apprenticeship, 1694–1708. 8vo, pp. xiii, (3), 678. New York, 1886.

Vol. XIX. 1886. Officers, 1887; Biographical notice of Silas Deane, by Charles Isham; The Deane Papers, Vol. I, 1774–1777. 8vo, pp. xiv, (2), 496. New York, 1887.

Vol. XX. 1887. Officers, 1888; The Deane papers, Vol. II, 1777–1778. 8vo, pp. (6), 499. New York, 1888.

Vol. XXI. 1888. Officers, 1889; The Deane papers, Vol. III, 1778–1779. 8vo, pp. (8), 490. New York, 1889.

Vol. XXII. 1889. Officers, 1890; The Deane papers, Vol. IV, 1779–1781. 8vo, pp. (8), 561. New York, 1890.

Vol. XXIII. 1890. Officers, 1891; The Deane papers, Vol. V, 1782–1790, 8vo. pp. 692. New York, 1891.

Vol. XXIV. 1891. Officers, 1892; Introduction; New York Muster Rolls, 1755–1764. 8vo, pp. xiii, 621. New York, 1892.

Vol. XXV. 1892. Officers; Introduction; Abstracts of Wills on file in the Surrogate's office, city of New York, Vol. I, 1665–1707. 8vo, pp. 520. New York, 1893.

Vol. XXVI. 1893. Officers; Abstracts of Wills, Vol, II, 1708–1728. With appendix and miscellaneous documents. 8vo, pp. 525. New York, 1894.

Vol. XXVII. 1894. Officers; Abstracts of Wills, Vol. III, 1729–1744; Letters of Administration, 1744; Appendix and miscellaneous papers. 8vo, pp. 501. New York, 1895.

Vol. XXVIII. 1895. Officers; Abstracts of Wills, Vol IV. 1744–

1753; Letters of Administration, 1745–1753. 8vo, pp. 559. New York, 1896.

Vol. XXIX. 1896. Officers; Abstracts of Wills, Vol. V, 1754–1760; Letters of Administration, 1753–1760. 8vo, pp. 496. New York, 1897.

Vol. XXX. 1897. Officers; Abstracts of Wills, Vol. VI, 1760–1766. Letters of Administration, 1760–1766. 8vo, pp. 517. New York, 1898.

Fitz Greene Halleck. A memorial. By F. S. Cozzens. Read before the Society, January 6, 1868. 8vo, pp. 32. New York, 1868.

The De Peyster Collection. Catalogue of books in the library of the Society, presented by John Watts De Peyster. Part I. January, 1868. 8vo, pp. 24. New York, 1868.

Catalogue of the museum and gallery of art of the Society, 1868. 8vo, pp. viii, 72, 61, (1). New York, 1868.

Circular letter. Museum of history, antiquities, and art in the Central Park, 4to, pp. 3. [New York, 1868.]

A narrative of events at Lake George, from the early colonial times to the close of the Revolution. By B. F. De Costa. 8vo, pp. 74. Large paper. New York, 1868.

Contains the substance of a paper read before the Society.

Catalogue of the museum and gallery of art of the Society, 1869. 8vo, pp. viii, 72, 61, (1). New York, 1869.

Historic progress and American democracy. An address delivered before the Society at their sixty-fourth anniversary, December 16, 1868. By John Lothrop Motley. 8vo, pp. (4), 74. New York, 1869.

Some notices of the life and writings of Fitz Greene Halleck. Read before the Society, February 3, 1869. By William Cullen Bryant. 8vo, pp. 43. New York, 1869.

Some recollections of the late Antoine Pierre Berryer. A paper read before the Society on February 16, 1869. By John Bigelow. 8vo, pp. (2), 36. [New York] 1869.

Catalogue of the museum and gallery of art of the Society, 1869. 8vo, pp. viii, 72, 61, (1). New York, 1869.

Same, 1870. New York, 1870.

Recent additions to the Bryan collection. 8vo, pp. 2. [New York, 1870.]

Beaumarchais, the merchant. Letters of Theveneau de Francey, 1777–1780. By John Bigelow. 8vo, pp. 16. New York, 1870.

Paper was partly read before the New York Historical Society, April 5, 1870.

A discourse on the life, character, and writings of Gulian Crommelin Verplanck. Delivered before the Society, May 17, 1870. By William Cullen Bryant. 8vo, pp. 60. New York, 1870.

Proceedings of the Society on the announcement of the death of Thomas J. Bryan, June 7, 1870. 8vo, pp. 10. New York, 1870.

Catalogue of the museum and gallery of art, 1871. 8vo, pp. iv, 72, 68. New York, 1871.

Memorial of Francis L. Hawks, D.D. By Evert A. Duyckinck. Read before the Society, May, 7, 1867. With an appendix of proceedings. 8vo, pp. 166. Portrait. New York, 1871.

The struggle for neutrality in America. An address delivered before the Society, at their sixty-sixth anniversary, December 13, 1870. By Charles Francis Adams. 8vo, pp. 52. New York, 1871.

A memorial of Alexander Anderson, M.D., the first engraver on wood in America. Read before the Society, October 5, 1870. By Benson J. Lossing. Large 8vo, pp. (6), 107. Illustrated, 23 plates, 38 woodcuts. Portraits. New York, 1872.

A memorial of Henry Theodore Tuckerman. By Evert A. Duyckinck. Read before the Society, January 2, 1872. With an appendix of proceedings. 8vo, pp. 15. Portrait. New York, 1872.

Incident in the war of the United States with Mexico, illustrating the services of William Maxwell Wood, Surgeon, U. S. N., in effecting the acquisition of California. By George C. McWhorter. Read before the Society, May 7, 1872. 8vo, pp. 10. [Oswego, N. Y., 1872.]

Memorial of John David Wolfe. Read before the Society, June 4, 1872. With a notice of proceedings. By Evert A. Duyckinck. 8vo, pp. 22. New York, 1872.

Why the early inhabitants of Vermont disclaimed the jurisdiction of New York and established an independent government. An address delivered before the Society, December 4, 1860. By Hiland Hall. 8vo, pp. 16. Bennington, 1872. Reprinted in 1884.

Catalogue of the museum and gallery of art of the Society, 1873. 8vo, pp viii, 72, 72. Woodcuts. New York, 1873.

The charter and by-laws. Revised January, 1858. With the amendments and a list of members. 8vo, pp. 39. New York, 1873.

A memorial of George Gibbs. By John Austin Stevens, jr. Read before the Society, October 7, 1873. With a notice of proceedings. 8vo, pp. 18. New York, 1873.

Address before the Society at the celebration of its sixty-ninth anniversary. January 6, 1874. On "William III as a reformer." By Frederic De Peyster. 8vo, pp. 36. New York, 1874.

Catalogue of the museum and gallery of art, 1874. 8vo, pp. iv, 72, 75. New York, 1874.

A memorial of Thomas De Witt, D.D. By Thomas E. Vermilye, D.D. Read before the Society, October 6, 1874. With a notice of proceedings. 8vo, pp. 28. New York, 1874.

The old streets of New York under the Dutch. Paper read before the Society, June 2, 1874. By James W. Gerard. 8vo, pp. 65. New York, 1874.
Same. 8vo, pp. 52. New York, 1875.

The charter and by-laws. Revised January, 1858. With the amendments and a list of members. 8vo, pp. 39. New York, 1875.

Maj. Gen. George H. Thomas. The annual address delivered before the

Society, January 5, 1875. By John Watts De Peyster. 8vo, pp. 24. New York, 1875.

The early American spirit and the genesis of it. Address before the Society at the celebration of its seventieth anniversary, April 15, 1875. By Richard S. Storrs. 8vo, pp. (2), 74. New York, 1875.

This paper was republished in 1878, with another on "The Declaration of Independence, and the effects of it."

The old Stadt Huys of New Amsterdam. Paper read before the Society, June 15, 1875. By James W. Gerard. 8vo, pp. 59. New York, 1875.

Thomas Crawford and art in America. Address before the Society, upon the reception of Crawford's statue of the Indian, presented by Frederic De Peyster, April 6, 1875. By Samuel Osgood, D.D. 8vo, pp. 40. New York, 1875.

Expedition of the Sieur De Champlain against the Onondagoes in 1615. Comprising an inquiry into the route of the expedition and the location of the Iroquois fort which it besieged. Communicated to the Society, October 5, 1875, by Orsamus H. Marshall. 8vo, pp. 18. New York, 1876.

This edition was suppressed and was followed by a new edition published in *Magazine of American History*, January, 1877. With title-page. 8vo, pp. 15. Map. New York, 1877.

Progress of New York in a century, 1776–1876. An address before the Society, December 7, 1875. By John Austin Stevens. 8vo, pp. 66. New York, 1876.

Nashville, the decisive battle of the Rebellion. [Address before the Society, January 4, 1876. By John Watts De Peyster.] 8vo, pp. 14. [New York, 1876.]

The battle of Harlem Plains. Oration, September 16, 1876. By John Jay. 8vo, pp. 84. New York, 1876.

Forms part of work entered below, entitled "The Commemoration of the Battle of Harlem Plains."

Commemoration of the battle of Harlem Plains on its one hundredth anniversary by the Society. 8vo, pp. 98. Plan. New York, 1876.

Pages 1–38 contain, with an independent title-page: "The Battle of Harlem Plains; oration, September 16, 1876, by John Jay." Pages 39–84 contain documentary matter relating to the same. [Compiled by William Kelby.] Pages 85–98, the proceedings of the Society in commemoration.

A biographical sketch of Robert R. Livingston. Read before the Society, October 6, 1876, by Frederic De Peyster. 8vo, pp. 38. Portrait. New York, 1876.

The New York delegates to the Continental Congress. By John Austin Stevens. Read before the Society, May 2, 1876. In the *Galaxy*, August, 1876.

The Huguenot element among the Dutch. By Ashbel G. Vermilye. Read before the Society, October 6, 1876. 8vo, pp. 23. Schenectady [1876].

Address before the Society at the celebration of its seventy-second anniversary, December 19, 1876. On "Representative men of the English revolution." By Frederic De Peyster. 8vo, pp. 44. Portraits. New York, 1876.

Catalogue of the museum and gallery of art, 1877. 8vo, pp. iv, 73, 78. New York, 1877.

The uniforms of the American army. By Asa Bird Gardiner. Read before the Society, November 7, 1876. Published in *Magazine of American History*, August, 1877. 8vo, 461–492, (1). New York, 1877.

The capture of Mount Washington, November 16, 1776, the result of treason. By Edward F. De Lancey. Read before the Society, December 5, 1876. 8vo, pp. 32. 2 maps. Reprint. New York, 1877.

Maj. Gen. Philip Schuyler and the Burgoyne campaign in the summer of 1771. The annual address, January 2, 1877, before the Society. By John Watts De Peyster. 8vo, pp. 26. New York, 1877.

Commemoration of the one hundredth anniversary of the adoption of the constitution of the State of New York. [April 20, 1777.] Address by Charles O'Conor, May 8, 1877. 8vo, pp. 40. New York, 1877.

Our national flag—the Stars and Stripes. Its history in a century. Read before the Society, June 14, 1877. Published in *Magazine of American History*, July, 1877. 8vo, pp. 401–428. New York, 1877.

The history of liberty, a paper read before the Society, February 6, 1866. By J. F. Aiken. With selected notes. 8vo, pp. 163. New York, 1877.

The globe of Vlpius, 1542. By B. F. De Costa. Read before the Society, December 4, 1877. Reprint. 32mo, pp. 8. [New York, 1878.]

The life, character, and writings of William Cullen Bryant. A commemorative address before the Society, at the Academy of Music, December 30, 1878. By George William Curtis. 8vo, pp. 64. New York, 1879.

The life and administration of Richard, Earl of Bellomont, governor of the provinces of New York, Massachusetts and New Hampshire from 1697 to 1701. An address before the Society at the celebration of its seventy-fifth anniversary, November 18, 1879. By Frederic De Peyster. 8vo, pp. (8), 59, (1), xvii. Facsimile. Portraits. New York, 1879.

History of New York during the Revolutionary war. By Thomas Jones. Edited by Edward F. De Lancey; with notes, contemporary documents, maps, and portraits. 8vo. Two volumes. The John Divine Jones Fund series of Histories and Memoirs. Printed for the Society. New York, 1879.

Memorial sketch of the life and literary labors of Evert Augustus Duyckinck. Read before the Society, January 7, 1879. By William Allen Butler. 8vo, pp. 16. Portrait. New York, 1879.

The battle of Harlem Heights, September 16, 1776. Read before the Society, February 5, 1878. With preface and notes. By Erastus C. Benedict. 8vo, pp. xi, 62. New York [1880].

Circular to members. 1880, 1881, 1882, 1883, and 1884. 4to. New York, 1880–1884.

Sir John Johnson, the first American-born baronet. An address delivered before the Society, January 6, 1880. By John Watts De Peyster. 8vo, pp. 24. New York, 1880.

"This contains the only trustworthy particulars of the battle of Oriskany, and a reprint, from the *Proceedings of the New Jersey Historical Society*, of a Diary," Vol. II, pp. 115–122, 127, 128.

Lady Deborah Moody. A discourse delivered before the Society, May 4, 1880. By James W. Gerard. Published, by permission of the author, by F. B. Patterson. 8vo, pp. 40. New York, 1880.

The charter and by-laws. Revised January, 1858. With the amendments and a list of members. 8vo, pp. 24. New York, 1881.

The battle or affair of King's Mountain, Saturday, October 7, 1780. Being the address delivered at the annual meeting of the Society, 4th of January, 1881. By John Watts De Peyster. 8vo, pp. 8. Half title. New York [1881].

The New York Continental Line of the army of the revolution. By Asa Bird Gardiner. Read before the Society. In *Magazine of American History*, December, 1881. 8vo, pp. 401–419. New York, 1881.

A memorial sketch of Frederic De Peyster, late president of the Society. Read October 3, 1882. [By Hamilton Fish.] Reprinted from the *Magazine of American History*, November, 1882. 4to, pp. 769–773. Portrait. New York, 1882.

Catalogue of the museum and gallery of art, 1883. 8vo, pp. iv, 73, 95. New York, 1883.

The impress of nationalities upon the City of New York. Read before the Society by James W. Gerard, May 1, 1883. 8vo, pp. 32. New York, 1883.

Memorial sketches of Stephen Whitney Phœnix. By Jacob B. Moore and Henry T. Drowne. Read before the Society, December 6, 1881, and before the Rhode Island Historical Society, July 3, 1883. 8vo, pp. 6, 7. Portrait. Reprint. Boston, 1883.

Resident members of the Society, March, 1884. 8vo, pp. 15. [New York, 1884.]

The peace negotiations of 1782 and 1783. An address before the New York Historical Society, November 27, 1883. By John Jay. 8vo, pp. 239. Map. New York, 1884.

Why the early inhabitants of Vermont disclaimed the jurisdiction of New York and established an independent government. An address delivered before the Society, December 4, 1860. By Hiland Hall. 8vo, pp. 15, (1). Bennington, Vt., 1872, and reprinted 1884.

Resolves, at meeting, March 4, 1884, on the death of Miss Eliza Susan Quincy. Broadside.

Report of Executive Committee, 1885, 1886, 1887, 1888, 1889, 1890, 1891, 1892, 1893, 1894, 1895, 1896, 1897, 1898, 1899, 1900, 1901, 1902, 1903. 8vo. New York, 1885–1903.

Catalogue of the museum and gallery of art, 1885. 8vo, pp. vii, 73, 95. New York, 1885.

Report of the joint committee on the centennial celebration of the evacuation of New York by the British, Monday, November 26, 1883. With an historical introduction, by John Austin Stevens. 4to, pp. 201. New York, 1885.

The Society had a principal part in the celebration, and was represented on the joint committee.

Final notes on witchcraft in Massachusetts. A summary vindication of the laws and liberties concerning attainders with corruption of blood, escheats, forfeitures for crime, and pardon of offenders, in reply to the "Reasons," etc., of Abner C. Goodell, jr. By George H. Moore. 8vo, pp. 120. New York, 1885.

Read in part before the Society, November 4, 1884.

The early New York post-office. Ebenezer Hazard, postmaster and postmaster-general. By Ashbel G. Vermilye, D.D. Read before the Society, December 2, 1884. In *Magazine of American History*, February, 1885. 8vo, pp. 113–130. New York, 1885.

The romantic school in American archæology. By Adolph F. Bandelier. Read before the Society, February 3, 1885. 8vo, pp. 14. New York, 1885.

Niagara's emancipation. Remarks of Luther Marsh, November 3, 1885, before the Society on reporting to it, as one of its committee, appointed to attend the opening ceremonies at the inauguration of the Niagara reservation, July 15, 1883. 8vo, pp. 18. New York, 1885.

Address on The Alphabet—The Vehicle of History, before the Society at its eighty-first anniversary, November 17, 1885. By Luther Marsh. 8vo, pp. 32. New York [1885].

Circular requesting subscriptions for new building, December 15, 1885. 4to, pp. 3.

Report on the gift to the Society of a copy of "State Trials of England," which originally belonged to Sir William Johnson, March 2, 1886. 8vo, pp. 4.

The first epic of our country. By the poet conquistador of New Mexico, Captain Gaspar De Villagra. By John Gilmary Shea. Read before the Society, March 2, 1886. 8vo, pp. 16. [New York, 1886.]

Resident members of the Society, May, 1886. 8vo, pp. 15. New York, 1886.

Leading incidents in the life of Henry Clay; his patriotism, statesmanship, and eloquence. An address by Erastus Brooks before the New York Historical Society, April 6, 1886, and before the Pennsylvania Historical Society, May 14, 1886. 8vo, pp. 32. New York, 1886.

Memorial notice of John B. Moreau. By Benson J. Lossing. Read before the Society, May 4, 1886. 12mo, pp. 12. [New York, 1886.]

Governor Thomas Pownall, Colonial statesman. By Robert Ludlow Fowler. Read before the Society, October 5, 1886. 8vo, pp. 20. Portrait. [New York, 1886.]

The opening, the use, and the future of our domain on this continent. An address before the Society on its eighty-second anniversary, November 16, 1886. By George E. Ellis, D.D. 8vo, pp. 34. New York, 1887.

Catalogue of the museum and gallery of art, 1887. 8vo, pp. vii, 73, 95. New York, 1887.

The framing of the Federal Constitution and the causes leading thereto. An address delivered before the Society on its eighty-third anniversary, Tuesday, November 15, 1887. By Hon. John Alsop King. 8vo, pp. 40. New York, 1888.

Appeal to the members and the citizens of New York for subscriptions to the building fund, December 14, 1887. 8vo, pp. 3.

Memorial to the Governor, the Senate and the Assembly of the State of New York. Centennial anniversary of the adoption by the State of New York of the Constitution of the United States (July 26, 1888). March 6, 1888. 4to, pp. 2.

The land politics of the United States. A paper read before the Society, Tuesday, May 1, 1888. By James C. Welling, LL.D. 8vo, pp. 40. New York, 1888.

Circular to the members of the Bar of the City of New York. Subscriptions to building fund. June 1, 1888. Broadside.

Circular letter to subscribers to the building fund, November 12, 1888. Broadside.

Some recollections of the late Édouard Laboulaye. By John Bigelow. 12mo, pp. (2), 81. [New York, 1888.]

A portion of these Recollections was read before the Society, November 20, 1888.

Frontenac and Miles Standish in the Northwest. A paper read before the Society, December 4, 1888. By Edward S. Isham. 8vo, pp. 39. New York, 1889.

The City of New York in the year of Washington's inauguration, 1789. By Thomas E. V. Smith. 8vo, pp. 244. Map. New York, 1889.

Read in part before the Society, February 5, 1889.

The progress of American independence. A paper read before the Society, April 2, 1889. By the Hon. George S. Boutwell. 8vo, pp. 31. New York, 1889.

An act to exempt the library edifice of the Society from sale under execution, June 13, 1889. 8vo, pp. 2. [New York, 1889.]

The uses of History. An address before the Society on its eighty-fifth anniversary, November 21, 1889. By John Hall, D.D. 8vo, pp. 27. New York, 1889.

The Kembles of New York and New Jersey, 8vo., pp. vii–xxiii. Portrait, Reprint of the prefatory note of volume xvii, collections of Society. [New York, 1889.]

The coaches of colonial New York. A paper read on the evening of March 4, 1890, before the Society. By George W. W. Houghton. 8vo, pp. 31. New York, 1890.

Connecticut federalism, or aristocratic politics in a social democracy. An address delivered before the Society on its eighty-sixth anniversary, Tuesday, November 18, 1890. By James C. Welling, LL.D. 8vo, pp. 43. New York, 1890.

Suum Cuique. John Dickinson, the author of the declaration on taking up arms in 1775. By George H. Moore, LL.D. Read before the Society, June 6, 1882. With a facsimile from the original draft. 8vo, pp. 53, (2), (8). New York, 1890.

Collegium Regale Novi Eboraci. The origin and early history of Columbia College. By George H. Moore, LL.D. Read before the Society, April 5, 1887. 8vo, pp. 46. New York, 1890.

Myvyrian Archæology. The Pre-Columbian voyages of the Welsh to America. By B. F. De Costa. Read before the Society, April 1, 1890. 8vo, pp. 12. Reprint, Albany, 1891.

Letter of committee on publications, February 23, 1891. 8vo, pp. 3. [New York, 1891.]

A monograph on the founding of Jersey City. By Charles H. Winfield. Read before the Society, June 2, 1891. 8vo, pp. 97. Portraits and plates. New York, 1891.

Resident members of the Society, January, 1892. 8vo, pp. 15. [New York, 1892.]

New York in 1850 and in 1890. A political study. An address delivered before the Society on its eighty-seventh anniversary, Tuesday, November 17, 1891, by the Hon. Seth Low, LL.D. 8vo, pp. 32. New York, 1892.

Appeal to the members and to the citizens of New York, January 19, 1892. 8vo, pp. 2. [New York, 1892.]

King George's personal policy in England. How it forced his subjects in America, against their wishes, into a successful revolution. By Edward F. De Lancey. Read before the Society, April 5, 1892. 8vo, pp. 431–448. [Reprint, New York, 1892.]

Columbian celebration of 1792. The first in the United States. An address before the Society, October 4, 1892. By Edward F. De Lancey. 8vo, pp. 18. Two portraits and four plates. Reprint. New York, 1893.

Catalogue of the museum and gallery of art, 1893. 8vo, pp. vii, 73, 98. New York, 1893.

Political parties and their places of meeting in New York City. By Thomas E. V. Smith. Read before the Society, February 7, 1893. 8vo, pp. 30. New York, 1893.

The siege of Cuantla, the Bunker Hill of Mexico. An address before the Society, April 4, 1893. By Walter S. Logan. 8vo, pp. 27. New York, 1893.

Circular letter of committee on the two hundredth anniversary of the introduction of the printing press in New York, April 5, 1893. 4to, pp. 3. [New York, 1893.]

Anneke Jans Bogardus and her farm. By James W. Gerard. Read before the Society, May 6, 1879. In *Harper's New Monthly*, May, 1885. 8vo, pp. 836–849. New York, 1885.

The Manor of Philipsburgh. A paper read before the Society, by T. Astley Atkins, June 5, 1894. 8vo, pp. 23. Yonkers, 1894. Published by the Yonkers Historical and Library Association.

Hopoghan Hackingh, Hoboken, a pleasure resort for old New York. By Charles H. Winfield, in two parts. Part II. read before the Society, December 4, 1894. 4to, pp. 80. Facsimile of Indian deed, July 12, 1630, and 8 plates. [New York, 1895.]

The charter and by-laws of the Society. Revised May, 1895. 8vo, pp. 24. New York, 1895.

The patriot clergy and the New York City chaplains in the War of the Revolution. An address before the Society, April 3, 1894, by Ashbel G. Vermilye, D.D., Board of Publication of the Reformed Church in America. 8vo, pp. 28. New York, 1895.

William Atwood, chief-justice of the colony of New York, 1701–1702. By Charles P. Daly, LL.D. Read before the Society, May 1, 1894. In the *Green Bag*, March–May, 1895, with additions.

Cabot and the transmission of English power in North America. An address before the Society on its ninety-second anniversary, November 18, 1896. By Justin Winsor, LL.D. 8vo, pp. 38. New York, 1896.

The establishment of public parks in the City of New York. By Gherardi Davis. Read before the Society, April 6, 1897. 12mo, pp. 46, (1). [New York, 1897.]

List of members of the Society, January, 1898. 8vo, pp. 14. [New York, 1898.]

The Palisades. By Ashbel G. Vermilye, D.D. Read before the Society, October 5, 1897. 8vo, pp. 335–350. Reprint.

A memoir of William Kelby, librarian of the Society. By John Austin Stevens. Read before the Society, November 1, 1898. 8vo, pp. 40. New York, 1898.

List of members of the Society, February, 1900. 8vo, pp. 14. [New York, 1900.]

Journalism in New York in 1800. A paper read before the Society, April 3, 1900. By Francis W. Halsey. In *The Journalist*, New York, April 7, 1900.

The old and the new century. An address before the Society on its ninety-sixth anniversary, November 20, 1900. By Marvin R. Vincent, D.D. 8vo, pp. 45. New York, 1900.

Memorial of the Hon. John Alsop King, eighteenth president of the Society. By the Very Rev. Eugene A. Hoffman, D.D. Read before the Society, February 5, 1901. 8vo, pp. 27. Portrait. New York, 1901.

Appendix to catalogue of gallery of art, 1894–1901. 8vo, pp. 3. [New York, 1901.]

Circular letters building committee, April 17 and November 4, 1901. 4to. Plates. [New York, 1901.]

Colonial homes in the Bronx. By Randall Camfort. Read before the Society, November 6, 1901. In Bronx Borough *Record*, October 21, 1901.

Letter of committee on membership, November 21, 1901. 4to, pp. 3. Plates. [New York, 1901.]

Before and after the treaty of Washington. The American Civil War and the war in the Transvaal. An address before the Society on its ninety-seventh anniversary, November 19, 1901. By Charles Francis Adams, LL.D. 8vo, pp. 141. New York, 1902.

John Pintard, founder of The New York Historical Society. An address before the Society, December 3, 1901. By James Grant Wilson. 8vo. pp. 37. Portrait. New York, 1902.

List of subscribers to the building fund, to December 31, 1901. 8vo, pp. 4, Plates. [New York, 1902.]

List of members of the Society, February, 1902. 8vo, pp. 15. New York, 1902.

Letter of committee on publications, February 15, 1902. 8vo, pp. 3. [New York, 1902.]

Communication to the members of the Society, from the building committee, February 15, 1902. Oblong 4to, pp. 13. Plates. [New York, 1902.]

Address commemorative of Eugene Augustus Hoffman. By William R. Huntington, D.D. Read before the Society, December 2, 1902. 8vo, pp. 28. Portrait. New York, 1903.

Memorial to the Governor, the Senate and Assembly of the State of New York, December, 2 1902. 4to, pp. 2.

List of members of the Society, February, 1903. 8vo, pp. 15. [New York, 1903.]

Catalogue of the museum and gallery of art, 1903. 8vo, pp. vii, 73, 102. New York, 1903.

The genius of the cosmopolitan city. An address before the Society on its ninety-ninth anniversary, November 17, 1903. 8vo, pp. 42. New York, 1904.

Charter, by-laws, officers, members, report of executive committee. 8vo, pp. 67. Plates. New York, 1904.

Banquet of the Society, November 22, 1904, in commemoration of the one hundredth anniversary of its founding. Menu, toasts, committee, views of homes of Society. 8vo, pp. 14. New York, 1904.

Seating plan, members and guests present at banquet, November 22, 1904. Broadside.

Letter of committee on anniversary medal, January 3, 1905. 8vo, pp. 2. Plate. [New York, 1905.]

The New York Historical Society, 1804–1904. By Robert H. Kelby. With appendix, list of officers and members, subscribers to building fund, funds of the Society, and bibliography. 8vo, pp. viii–160. 5 Plates. Facsimile of minutes of the Society, November 20, 1804; Portraits of founders; Homes of the Society; Portraits of Presidents, 1805–1849 and 1850–1905; Portrait of Henry Dexter. Printed for the Society. New York, 1905.

www.ingramcontent.com/pod-product-compliance
Lightning Source LLC
LaVergne TN
LVHW010606110826
845149LV00003B/794

* 9 7 8 1 4 1 8 1 8 7 3 9 2 *